HIKING SIPSEY

HISTORY OF A FAMILY'S FIGHT FOR WILDERNESS IN BANKHEAD NATIONAL FOREST

RICKEY BUTCH WALKER

JIM MANASCO

This work is based from the author's personal research and interpretation.

Managing Editor — Angela Broyles
Interior Design — Katie Warren
Cover Design — David Walker

OTHER BOOKS BY RICKEY BUTCH WALKER

Cotton Was King – Franklin – Colbert County – Alabama Plantation Series, ISBN: 978-1-949711-08-0, $24.95

Cotton Was King - Lauderdale County – Alabama Plantation Series, ISBN: 978-1-934610-99-2, $24.95

Cotton Was King - Lawrence County – Alabama Plantation Series, ISBN: 978-1-949711-14-1, $24.95

Cotton Was King - Limestone County – Alabama Plantation Series, ISBN: 978-1-949711-35-6, $24.95

Cotton Was King - Morgan County – Alabama Plantation Series, ISBN: 978-1-958273-03-6, $29.95

Appalachian Indians of the Warrior Mountains: History and Culture, ISBN: 978-1-934610-72-5, $24.95

Appalachian Indian Trails of the Chickamauga: Lower Cherokee Settlements, ISBN: 978-1-934610-91-6, $24.95

Celtic Indian Boy of Appalachia: A Scots Irish Cherokee Childhood, ISBN: 978-1-934610-75-6, $24.95

Chickasaw Chief George Colbert: His Family and His Country, ISBN: 978-1-934610-71-8, $24.95

Doublehead: Last Chickamauga Cherokee Chief, ISBN: 978-1-958273-09-8, $24.95

Soldier's Wife: Cotton Fields to Berlin and Tripoli, ISBN: 978-1-9582730-98, $19.95

Warrior Mountains Folklore: American Indian and Celtic History in the Southeast, ISBN: 978-1-934610-65-7, $29.95

Warrior Mountains Indian Heritage-Teacher's Edition, ISBN: 978-1-934610-27-5, $39.95

Warrior Mountains Indian Heritage-Student Edition, ISBN: 978-1-934610-66-4, $24.95

Black Folk Tales of the Shoals, ISBN: 978-1-958273-07-04, $24.95

ACKNOWLEDGEMENTS

I want to thank my longtime friend Jim Manasco and his family for all their help with Hiking Sipsey; Jim is an exceptional and awesome writer. He has a wonderful way of using words; it was a pleasure to co-author this personal view of our Sipsey River drainage. Without Jim's enlightening words and remarkable experiences, Hiking Sipsey would not be possible.

Most people take the Sipsey Wilderness Area for granted, but Jim and Ruth Manasco including many other people and organizations mounted a very stressful fight to save the area that span some 15 years. One of the strongest opponents to wilderness was the United States Forest Service and the corporate timber industry that waged an ugly demeaning campaign in order to clear cut the whole forest; without the stand of Jim and Ruth Manasco along with grassroots efforts and organizations, we would not have the Sipsey Wilderness Area for the world to enjoy.

I want to thank my dear friend Wheeler Pounds for editing the final manuscript and writing an exceptional book review. Wheeler and I have been friends many years and hiked wonderful places throughout the Sipsey drainage.

I also want to thank David Walker for his work in the completion of Hiking Sipsey. David is a graphic artist and did an outstanding job in designing the cover of the book. David is a friend who shares a deep love for all the old trails of our aboriginal past.

Lamar Marshall is a great friend; he provided pictures and the interview with Jim Manasco that has made this book much better. Lamar also provided photos of the original Sipsey Wilderness Area map that is now in the Alabama Archives in Montgomery, Alabama.

Table of Contents

INTRODUCTION

Many people fought to preserve wilderness areas in the eastern United States, but one family dedicated a large portion of their lives to protect an area they learned to love as mixed-blood Cherokee children growing up with families that lived in the Sipsey River area of North Alabama. Jim and Ruth Manasco were children of mixed-blood Cherokee Indian families whose ancestors called the Sipsey area home; they taught their children to love the forest of their aboriginal heritage. Their families survived in the upper hill country of the Black Warrior Mountains which are the highlands that drain into the Black Warrior River Basin. The Jim and Ruth Manasco family struggled for the preservation and protection of their childhood stomping grounds; through their efforts, they helped preserve thousands of acres of wilderness across the eastern portion of the United States.

Long before Jim and Ruth ever met, their mixed Cherokee families had instilled a love for the beautiful and serene canyons of Sipsey River flowing through the present-day William B. Bankhead National Forest. Their families knew that the canyons had been formed from a thousand waterfalls that created the eternal sounds of wilderness as they cascaded from sandstone bluffs into the streams entering Sipsey River.

Early in their childhood, the forest was playing a major role in their development as their families were utilizing the Sipsey for their survival and wellbeing; however, the timber industry began taking their old growth forest at an alarming rate. This was a land that Jim and Ruth knew and loved so that destruction of its old growth was not an option; it was to them and still

Jim and Ruth Manasco at old growth beech

is the Black Warrior Forest even though the name was changed to recognize a white politician known as William B. Bankhead.

In the 1960s, their precious and beloved forest they knew as mixed Native American Indian children was being attacked by the very people who were supposed to be its protectors; the forest was being sold to the timber companies and dismantled by the United States Forest Service in the form of clear cutting and conversion of old growth hardwood forests into commercial pine plantations. Sipsey River along with feeder streams were being filled with silt from extreme timber harvesting and pine stand conversion activities; many rare and endangered plants and animals were being adversely impacted and affected by the actions of an out of control big government agency driven by politically powerful timber corporations. These actions by a government bureaucracy were totally unacceptable to Jim and Ruth Manasco.

Jim and Ruth Manasco started the biggest fight of their lives which culminated in the preservation of Sipsey Wilderness Area. Other eastern wildernesses in United States were created by being piggy backed on the Sipsey Bill introduced by Senator John Sparkman of Hartselle, Alabama. Ruth said, "*Wilderness is the most important thing I ever done except having children!*"

> **Wilderness is the most important thing I ever done except having children!**

Jim, Ruth, and their children Tim, Rusty, and Terra sacrificed their time and energy to protect the sacred grounds their ancestors had walked for thousands of years before the coming of white man. For years, the Manascos spent three days per week walking, photographing, writing, and trying to draw attention to the plight of the Sipsey River canyons; this was one family's fight to save and protect the Sipsey area that they had been taught to love as children and knew as the Black Warrior.

Manasco Family-Rusty, Jim, Ruth, Terra, and Tim

Black Warrior

DeSoto and Tuscaloosa

Jim and Ruth wanted to honor their Native American ancestors by naming the Sipsey River area they were struggling to protect and preserve the Black Warrior Wilderness. From the early 1730s, the French explorers, trappers, and traders had referred to this upper drainage area of the Black Warrior River by its Indian name Riverie de Tuscaloosa; in Muskogee (Creek Indian) language, *tusca* means warrior with *loosa* meaning black and the words together are warrior black.

Jim and Ruth felt that it was fitting to call the Sipsey old growth forest they were trying to preserve the Black Warrior Wilderness. The Manasco Family knew that the great Creek Chief Tuscaloosa at one time controlled the area of Sipsey River; in 1540, Tuscaloosa and his people fought DeSoto and his Spanish conquistadors.

In addition, Creek Indian lands lay to the south of the High Town Path that followed along the Tennessee Divide while the Chickasaw and Cherokee lands lay north of the path; the divide also defined the northern boundary of the Sipsey River drainage basin. As Governor of Southwest Territory, William Blount in a 1794 letter to the chiefs and headmen of the Creek Indians said, *"In the original division of land amongst the red people, it is well known that the Creek lands were bounded on the north by the ridge which divides the waters of the Mobile and the Tennessee;"* Southwest Territory was defined as that area of land that lay south of the Ohio River and west of the Appalachian Mountains. The Chickasaw Boundary as defined at the Treaty of Hopewell on January 10, 1786, ran along the High Town Path that followed the Tennessee Divide through William B. Bankhead National Forest.

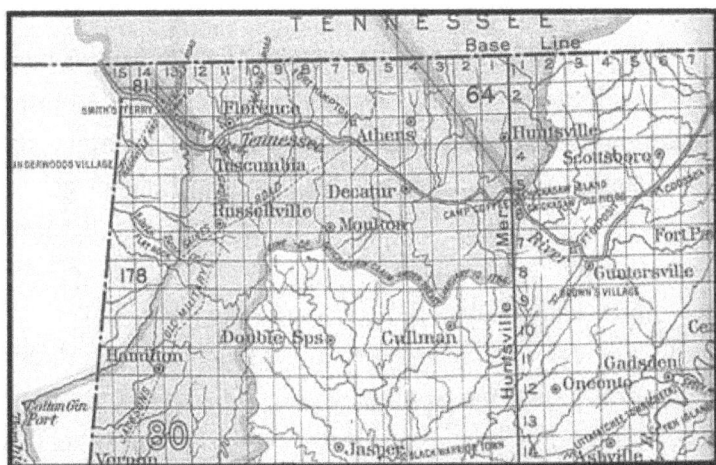

High Town Path-Chickasaw Boundary 1/10/1786
18th Annual Report, Bureau of American Ethnology

The present-day Ridge Road, Leola Road, and portions of the Cheatham Road and Byler Road in Bankhead Forest follow the Tennessee Divide and High Town Path which was the northern boundary of the Creek Indian Nation; water flowing south of this line goes into the Sipsey River and then into the Black Warrior River; the water to the north of these roads drains into the Tennessee River, then the Ohio River, and to the Mississippi River. The water to the south of these roads and the Tennessee Divide flows into streams feeding Sipsey River, then to the Mulberry Fork of the Warrior River, and eventually into Mobile Bay.

At one time, the upper Sipsey woodlands were named the Black Warrior Forest; the name was eventually changed to honor a white United States Congressman by the name of William B. Bankhead. Today, the hunting area is controlled by the State of Alabama Department of Conservation and Natural Resources and is called the Black Warrior Wildlife Management Area; the wildlife management area encompasses the Sipsey Wilderness Area.

After deciding on the name of Black Warrior for this new eastern wilderness they were seeking to preserve for future generations to enjoy, Jim and Ruth faced another dilemma; the Black Panther organization became a radical militant group and congressional approval may have been swayed by the close association in the names. In order not to create a huge controversy in the United States Congress over the name, Jim reluctantly said, "*Just call the area the Sipsey Wilderness;*" thus, the name of the area came from the Creek Indian word meaning poplar or cotton wood tree and to this day is known as the Sipsey Wilderness Area. Jim personally took an original map and some 350,000 letters of endorsement for the Sipsey Wilderness Area to Washington, D.C.

Jim Manasco realizes the fights to save his sacred aboriginal lands of Sipsey River are not over. Corporate and industrial interests want the coal, oil, gas, and other minerals that lay under the Black Warrior Mountains and the Sipsey area of Bankhead Forest. The future is not certain; we all must stay diligent to ensure our wilderness is protected from future attempts to harvest the mineral rights.

JIM MANASCO

Jim Manasco at Oakville

Jim was the fourth child of five siblings; the Manasco children were Betty, Frances, Bob, Jim, and Bill. All of Jim's brothers and sisters earned college degrees; Jim went to college at Florence one year. Jim's parents were Joseph (Joe) Viletus Manasco and Bertha Mae Simms; Jim's family owned a little cabin in the Sipsey drainage and he grew up rambling around the Bankhead Forest from childhood.

Jim's father Joseph V. Manasco was born on December 12, 1894, and died on January 8, 1975. Joseph was the son of Caleb Riley Manasco (11/19/1869–7/4/1925) and Dialphia Hyde (1871–1960); Caleb was born in Lynn, Alabama, to Archibald Richard Manasco and Amanda Tucker; he died at Lynn, Alabama, in Winston County; Lynn was originally known as the Old Black Swamp.

Joseph was a telegraph operator for the railroad at Lynn; he was featured in a magazine as the only man to send and receive Morse code at the same time. Joseph served in the United States Army during World War I from 1917–1918.

Jim's father was a mail carrier on rural route two; Jim loved animals and his dad would bring orphan animals to Jim. He would nourish and take care of these forest babies until they were strong and well enough to make it on their own; Jim kept animals all his life! He was given every kind of animal that was left in mailboxes. Rural route two of the Carbon Hill Post Office covered the southern part of Walker County; many of his baby animals came from the Berry Community in Fayette County and the Sipsey drainage.

Jim's maternal grandparents were Garret Dodd and Roxanna Kizzar Sims. After Kizzy's husband Garrett Dodd was killed on the railroad, she opened a general store to make a living. Jim was delivered into this world by his grandmother Roxanna Kizzar (Kizzy) Sims; he was born on December 18, 1933, in saw mill camp house in Eldridge, Alabama. Eldridge was named after the son-in-law of John Byler who built the first state road in Alabama; the road was authorized on December 16, 1819, only two days after Alabama became a state. Today, the western boundary of the Sipsey Wilderness Area follows portions of Byler's Old Turnpike in the Kinlock portion of the forest.

Manasco Family

Jim says, "*Manasco was knighted by Charla-Mane or Charla Magne from Bask to the south of France. The original Manascos of my family were French mercenaries who eventually migrated to America in the early 1700s.*" According to Ancestry.com, John Manasco, a direct ancestor to Jim, was born in 1716 in the French-controlled Louisiana in what is present-day United

States of America. Some say the Manascos were from Wales which could be due to the Norman invasion accounting for the French in Great Britain.

Joseph Manasco's great-grandfather was David Manasco, who was born about 1802 and died in 1884; David was married four times and had 17 children. David Manasco's family lived on Payne Creek in Bankhead Forest; the creek was named in honor of Matthew Payne, only one of two Revolutionary War soldiers buried in Winston County, Alabama. Matthew is buried in the Payne-Robbins Cemetery on the south side of Caney Creek of the Sipsey River drainage and west of the mouth of Payne Creek; the cemetery is just a few miles south and downstream from the present-day Sipsey Wilderness Area.

Joseph V. Manasco owned some 300 acres of land north from Sipsey River along Highway 33 and upstream from the mouth of Payne Creek. The Manasco Family has a long history in the Sipsey River area of Winston County, Alabama; the family has lived in the area for over 200 years.

Jim is a Cherokee Indian artist; he has always been proud of his Cherokee Indian ancestry. Jim has completed several oil paintings on canvas; his portraits and drawings represent different aspects of his Cherokee Indian background, culture, and heritage. Jim got his artistic ability from a family lineage of artisans.

Joseph V. Manasco's entire family was into art. Joseph's brother, Robert or Rupbert, was ragtime piano player; he could play piano like a master, but had no training in music. Another brother, Grady, was General Manager of St. Joe Paper Company. Aubrey Manasco was a musician and sorted mail at the post office; he would slip away from work and play music in church. Lee Sr. taught music (sacred harp), and was a conductor on a passenger train; the train had layovers at Lynn, Alabama. Cousin Lee Malone Jr., the son of Joseph's sister, had a radio station by age of 16; he was in guidance and control at Marshall Space Flight Center.

Joseph (Joe) V. Manasco wrote journals and memoirs; his notes are in the Double Springs archives. He carried mail as part of the Pony Express with two horses and flatbed wagon from Lynn to the post office in Double Springs. Joe started working on the mail route when he was 16 years old; he got the job carrying mail after working in freight at Carbon Hill, Alabama. After delivering mail, Joseph started working with the railroad; he worked for the railroad until he was disabled.

Bertha, Jim's mother, had a sister, Calantha, that lived in Denver, Colorado. Calantha had tuberculosis while living in Alabama and was told by her doctor to move to Colorado. She lived to be a ripe old age because of the dry climate. Prior to Jim's birth, his parents went west to visit his Aunt Calantha; Jim's father Joe got a job with the D & R Railroad (Denver and Royal Gorge Western) on September 2, 1926. Joseph was a telegraph operator for the railroad at Royal Gorge, Colorado. He was the only employee on the Rio Grande River during his two day shift. While working in the Royal Gorge, Joseph trained mice to amuse him.

One day after Joseph had turned the duties over to his replacement to take a break, the guy got drunk and failed to send the oncoming trains the message to side track. Trains were on a collision course; when Joseph returned, he saw the guy was drunk. Joseph walked down the track in efforts to stop the trains, but his efforts were in vain; he could not get the trains to stop. The two trains collided head on in the Royal Gorge in 1926; after the train crash, Joseph Manasco came back to Alabama and settled in the Sipsey River drainage.

Sims and Engle Family

Bertha Sims, Jim's mother, was a housewife, but could do about anything she wanted to such as playing music with a violin. Jim said, "*Mother was not sweetest person in the world.*" Bertha's mother was Roxanna Engle and her father was Marion Dodd Simms; the Simms family came from New York to North Alabama. Marion Dodd Simms lived in the Community of Manchester near Blackwater Creek; he worked for the railroad and hauled out old natural growth long leaf pines which were found in this area.

> **Mother was not the sweetest person in the world!**

The Engle Family lived at Ashbank near the railroad; Roxanna told Jim about his Cherokee Indian bloodlines, but many times she called her family Black Dutch in order to cover her Cherokee Indian identity. Roxanna was 5/16 Cherokee; she was the daughter of Paul Engle who was 5/8 Cherokee. Paul Engle's mother was full Cherokee and her name was

Rebecca Catherine Tittle
1823-1894

Ruth; Paul was the son of John Engle. John was the oldest son of Peter Engle, who was one half Cherokee; Peter and his dad Andrew Jackson Engle founded the Town of Double Springs, Alabama.

Andrew Jackson Engle was the father of Peter Engle; Andrew Jackson Engle was married to Rebecca Catherine Tittle who was Cherokee Indian. It is thought that Jim Tittle was her father and came from east Tennessee to Old Black Swamp (Lynn).

The Tittle family initially came into the Cherokee Nation area during the 1750s when the Chickamauga faction of the Lower Cherokee claimed the Tennessee River Valley and the Coosa River Valley portion of North Alabama. Today, descendants of the Tittle family still reside in the area of the Sipsey River drainage.

Andrew Jackson Engle

Andrew Jackson Engle was born in Jefferson County, Alabama, on January 20, 1820, and died in Winston County, Alabama, at Double Springs in 1896; he became a merchant in Eldridge, Walker County, Alabama, prior to moving to Double Springs. Andrew was a strong Union sympathizer during the Civil War and aided Union sol-

Andrew Jackson Engle
1820-1896

diers with money, food, and other provisions; he informed the Union forces about the location of the Confederate troops.

13

Andrew was the first man in Alabama to be arrested for disloyalty to the Confederacy; he was arrested by the Confederate forces on several occasions and held and questioned. On many occasions, Rebel guards were posted at his house to prevent him informing the Union forces of Rebel locations.

Andrew Jackson Engle persuaded some of his neighbors to join the Union Army; he helped their families while they were away by supplying them with food and cultivating their fields. In 1863, Andrew Jackson Engle was elected as County Commissioner by his Union followers in Winston County and served about a year and half.

To prevent being conscripted by the Confederate Army, Andrew served as a guard for the Confederate mail from Tuscaloosa to Courtland, Alabama, for about three months in 1864-65. The main mail route to Courtland was along the Cheatham Road which was initially an old Indian path known as the Sipsie Trail. The Cheatham Road that passed through Moulton, Alabama, became Highway 33; today the road runs along a portion of the present-day Sipsey Wilderness Area in Bankhead National Forest.

Confederate General Phillip Dale Roddy of Moulton, Alabama, camped on Andrew Jackson Engle's place for

Major General James Harrison Wilson

14

about two weeks in 1863, consuming the entire products of his plantation and taking some of his livestock, for which he received no pay. Again in 1865, Major General James Harrison Wilson's mounted cavalry made their raid through North Alabama during which some of Andrew Jackson Engle's property was seized by the Union Army. Major General James Harrison Wilson was a 27-year-old boy general of the Union. Prior to taking Andrew's property, General Harrison's army camped at Clear Creek Falls; the falls became historically important during the Civil War as a result of the Union Army campsite. Today, Jim and Ruth live within a short distance of the old falls which are now flooded by Smith Lake. The falls of Clear Creek were also a major landmark to the Indians and early settlers of the area.

Kinlock Falls at Hubbard's Mill

According to the *Annals of Northwest Alabama* by Carl

Elliott published in 1972, Major General James H. Wilson formed the world's largest cavalry of 13,480 mounted Union soldiers at Gravely Springs in Lauderdale County, Alabama. The Union troops were armed with Spencer repeating rifles, and they were riding some of the best horses in the country. After being split in Lauderdale County into three units, the brigades of Wilson's army united and camped near Clear Creek Falls on March 25, 1865.

One brigade of the Yankees of Northern Aggression traveled by way of Byler's Old Turnpike to Kinlock Falls and Hubbard's Mill in Lawrence County, Alabama. The Union division camped around Kinlock Spring at David Hubbard's home place on March 24, 1865, before uniting with the rest of Wilson's command at Clear Creek Falls on the following day. Some of the Wilson's Union divisions passed through and by the present-day Sipsey Wilderness Area and William B. Bankhead National Forest.

Wilson's Union army went from Clear Creek Falls to capture Selma, Alabama, on April 2, 1865, and four other fortified cities in Alabama including Birmingham and Montgomery. On Easter Day on April 16, 1865, Wilson's army captured Columbus, Georgia, which was considered the last major battle of the Civil War. During May 1865, Wilson's army captured Confederate President Jefferson Davis as he was fleeing through Georgia.

After the Civil War, Andrew Jackson Engle filed a claim containing numerous affidavits from several people stating his loyalty to the Union and for payment for his property taken by General Roddy and Major General Wilson. The Committee on War Claims of the United States House of Representatives, on the grounds that he must have taken an allegiance to the Confederacy to have held the position of mail guard and county commissioner, refused his claims even though Commissioner J.B. Powell in Washington, D.C. stated that such an office did not require allegiance to the Confederacy.

Upper and Lower Clear Creek Falls

Andrew and his son Peter are considered the founders of Double Springs, Alabama; Andrew moved from Eldridge to Double Springs after the Civil War. At Double Springs, Andrew started a mercantile business; he was elected State Representative in 1875. In 1882, Andrew was elected to the State Constitutional Convention; he was also one of the leaders in establishing Engles Mill which later became known as Nauvoo Mill.

Roxanna and Moon

Roxanne Engle Simms (the great-great-granddaughter of Andrew Jackson Engle) was Jim's grandmother; Jim lived with his grandma Roxanna during the summer months. Roxanne always wore a Cherokee medicine bag pinned to her apron; Jim's daughter, Terra, ended up with the medicine bag. Jim told about his grandmother Roxanna's family being friends to a Cherokee Indian by the name of Moon; Jim said, "*I never heard him called anything but Moon or Mr. Moon.*"

Moon was a Cherokee Indian from Oklahoma and a friend of Roxanna's family; Moon would come to Alabama to visit with Roxanna and her family. Jim said, "*My love for forest and Sipsey River area came from Uncle Aubrey Sims who treated me like an adult. Moon, Uncle Aubrey Simms, and Jack Harris were close friends; they would take Moon fishing using hand caught crickets and cane poles. All the men would be drinking heavy and usually catching fish; they loved their wildcat whiskey.*"

Since the Oklahoma Cherokee Indian liked to fish, Jim would take Moon to his favorite fishing spot on Blackwater Creek. Jim was fishing with Moon the day he committed suicide in a boat in Blackwater Creek; at the time, Jim was about 12 years old. Jim said, "*One day, I was paddling Mr. Moon down the creek when he told me to pull the boat up to bank; he told me to go to house which was a few hundred yards away and tell Roxanna to come to the creek. I went to the house as instructed and told my grandma Roxanna that Mr. Moon was at the creek and that she needed to see about him. When we got back to the boat, Mr. Moon had shot himself in the head and was dead; Grandma Roxanna called the sheriff. Moon had come from Oklahoma and committed suicide after fishing with me; Mr. Moon had been deeply involved in Indian hierarchy."*

Jim said, *"Uncle Aubrey Sims and his friend Jack Harris never did do well, but made out and survived; neither one of them ever had permanent jobs. Aubrey and Jack lived and camped in the forest; they had both a winter camp and summer camp in the Sipsey River area and spent most of their lives in the forest. Aubrey and Jack's primary occupation was making moonshine whiskey; every time they would go to the woods and I followed along.*

Aubrey and Jack would make their beds by placing four poles about two feet off the ground under a rock shelter; the horizontal poles was then be covered with chicken wire; the chicken wire would be overlaid with hemlock branches. They would sleep under bluffs on these hemlock beds above the ground; the chicken wire with hemlock branches slept great and smelled good. The men slept in the sags of the wire and were very comfortable.

They made their own fishing boats; they got lumber to build boats from the local sawmill. The boat was made with two fourteen foot long oak boards that were one inch thick by twelve inches wide planks for the sides; three of the same boards for the floor; and, one board for the seat. In other words, it took six boards to make boat; Texas Star duplicated the old Blackwater flat boat!"

> **I was an expert on Blackwater Creek before I had social skills to get a hamburger!**

Jim said, *"At 16 years of age, I was an expert on Blackwater Creek before I had social skills to get hamburger!"*

Jim and his cousin L. G.

19

Dodd also made a metal boat out of car parts; the car hood was the bow of the boat and the top was the main body of the boat which was spot welded. They placed two boards in the middle for seats; their homemade metal canoe was put in Sipsey River at the picnic ground on the Cranal Road. Jim and L. G. put out trot lines filled with bait and caught a bunch of catfish. Their masterfully crafted boat eventually sunk!

RUTH CASTLEBERRY MANASCO

Ruth's parents were Arthur L. Castleberry (12/7/1889–11/14/1970) and Nancy Pearl Estelle Sides (2/9/1894–8/10/1982); Arthur and Nancy are buried in the Smith Chapel Cemetery at Carbon Hill in Walker County, Alabama. Ruth's father was a miner. Ruth was born at home on June 24, 1937, three miles north of Carbon Hill, Alabama. The family lived in the Smith Chapel Community about three miles north of Carbon Hill; Ruth went to Prospect Junior High and graduated from the ninth grade.

Ruth was the youngest of seven children; they are Millard Castleberry, Vertie Mae Masterson, Robenia (Robbie) Castleberry, S. W. (Woody) Castleberry, Donald (Don) Castleberry, Helen Smith, and Ruth. Her brother Woody, presently 90 years old, was 16 years old when Ruth was born; he knew that his dad went to get a doctor. Woody sneaked back to see what was going on at his house; he came home to find his new baby sister Ruth.

Ruth's maternal grandparents were Jefferson (Jeff) Thomas Sides (11/6/1864–9/16/1941) and Sarah Frances Morgan Sides (8/6/1870–

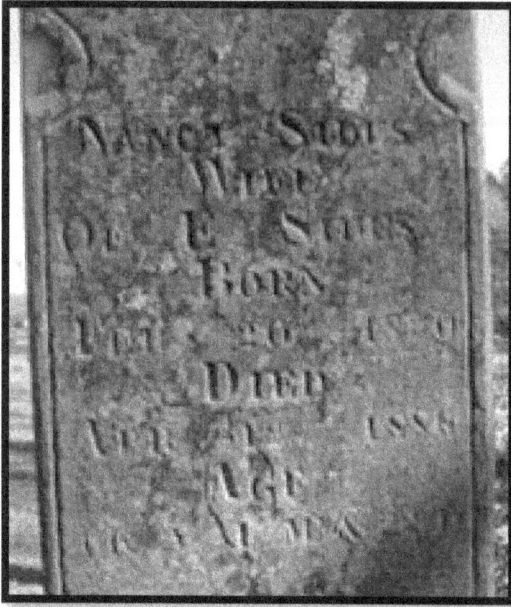

8/14/1944); Jefferson and Sarah Sides are buried in the Smith Chapel Cemetery at Carbon Hill in Walker County, Alabama. Ruth's Cherokee grandfather Jefferson Thomas Sides gave her family the 20 acre home place where Ruth was born.

Jeff's parents were Elijah Sides and Nancy Brown; Elijah and Nancy were married on February 3, 1843. Elijah was the son of Henry Sides (1/9/1779–1/15/1867) and Sarah Susanna Ashcraft (8/30/1788–9/26/1874). Elijah was born on January 4, 1824, in Walker County, Alabama; he died on March 28, 1900, and is buried in the Old Zion Cemetery on Alabama Highway 5, a few miles west of Jasper, Alabama.

Nancy Brown Sides was born on February 2, 1820, in Walker County, Alabama; she died April 12, 1886, and is also buried in the Old Zion Cemetery west of Jasper. Nancy's parents were John M. "Cherokee Jack" Brown (1780–7/3/1845) and Hannah Rice (3/10/1780–1852). Elijah and Nancy had four children: John Ruben Sides (1850–1923); David Wolfe Sides (1852-1930); Martha Sides Myers (1860–1924); and Jefferson Thomas Sides.

Jeff's Cherokee Indian blood came from his mother Nancy Brown (1/4 Cherokee), his grandfather John M. "Cherokee Jack" Brown (1/2 Cherokee), and Cherokee Chief John Lucian Brown (full Cherokee). John M. Brown and Hannah Rice had two daughters who were Nancy Hannah Brown Sides and Sarah Brown Ellis (9/30/1829–5/18/1889); Sarah was married to Jim Ellis and is buried in Shiloh Cemetery on the Marigold Road, a few miles north of Jasper, Alabama.

Jeff and Sarah Sides

On March 20, 1907, Jefferson Thomas Sides filed an application with the Commissioner of Indian Affairs in Washington, D. C., for a share of the fund appropriated by Act of Congress approved June 30, 1906, in accordance with the decrees of Court of Claims of May 18, 1905 and May 28, 1906, in favor of the Eastern Cherokees. Again on July 2, 1907, Jefferson Thomas Sides submitted an application for his minor children; his original application number was 21347. In both applications, Jeff T. Sides provided sworn affidavits with appropriate witnesses; however, his application was rejected. The rejected application did not mean that Jeff T. Sides was not of Cherokee Indian ancestry; many applications of Cherokee ancestry were rejected based only on the lack of Dawes or Guion Miller roll numbers. Mixed-blood Indian people that remained in Alabama after the 1838 removal could not legally identify themselves as Indian; therefore, they did not receive enrollment numbers. Jeff T. Sides tried for some two years to get his application approved, but was not successful.

Ruth's family kept all the court documents presented by her grandfather to the Indian Affairs in Washington; these records verify that the family was of Cherokee ancestry. Ruth is proud of her Cherokee blood and has been very active in her Dancing Rabbit Studio; she makes beautiful Cherokee Indian pottery.

JIM AND RUTH MANASCO

Ruth knew Jim from his dad being a mail carrier. Jim's younger sister, Xan Carol Manasco, and Ruth became best friends in tenth grade at Carbon Hill High School. Ruth would go home with Xan; she was responsible for Ruth and Jim's first date or visitation. Through the friendship, Jim and Ruth got to know each other and made a companionship that will last their lifetimes.

An ancestral thread tied both Jim and Ruth to the Bankhead Forest that they loved as their families before them. Jim was 21 and Ruth was 18 years old when they married July 8, 1955. Jim's sister Frances planned their marriage. Ruth and Jim eloped in Betty Jo's borrowed car and got married in Tupelo, Mississippi; they did not have to have a blood test in Mississippi.

Jim and Ruth were blessed with

Mark Ruston Manasco

three children: Tim was born August 21, 1957; Rusty was born April 20, 1960, and died June 23, 2007; and Terra was born July 19, 1963! Ruth and Jim had incompatible blood types; Terra was born with jaundice and turned a yellow color the day after she was born. When her blood number got to 16 they would change blood but after it got to 15, the number started dropping; therefore, Jim and Ruth survived the scare and had a healthy baby girl.

Jim and Ruth's oldest son Tim (James Timothy Manasco) was a born naturalist; he caught, identified, and turned loose every living creature in the forest. At one point when he returned from Boy Scout Camp, Tim got a ride home to Clear Creek with one of our good friends Mike Hopiak and his friend Bryan Stovall. They were talking about the flattened musk turtle being found in the Bankhead National Forest; they described it as having a flattened back. The next weekend he went over to Great Uncle Dodd's fishing marina and found a flattened musk turtle in his minnow trap. He was the most excited as we had ever seen him; it was quite a big discovery to find in Clear Creek of Smith Lake the flattened musk turtle, *Sternothaures depressus*.

Jim and Ruth's son Mark Ruston Manasco was following in Tim's every step. Ruth said, "*We led so many field trips to identify the plants, animals, reptiles, amphibians, birds, plants, and various flora and fauna. The children went along on most of these field trips. They got to meet so many people, from locals who cared deeply for the forest and did not want to see clear cutting continue, a lot of State and Federal dignitaries, and a lot of wildlife biologists who were well known outside the area of Bankhead National Forest. Rusty went on to work in various fields, but ended with his favorites, jewelry making and gun smithing. Our*

Terra Manasco

son, Mark Ruston Manasco, passed away in June 2007."

The youngest child was Terra L. Manasco; she got a degree from Auburn University in Wildlife science, not too surprising; then a few years later she got a degree from IAIA in Santa Fe, New Mexico, in pottery. She followed in the steps of her artist father and the love of the earth from our whole family.

Terra still has the ceremonial Cherokee pipe that came down through several generations from Drowning Bear (Yonaguska or John Brown). John Brown had the ceremonial pipe that was passed to him through many generations; after John adopted Will Thomas, he passed the pipe to Will. Will Thomas passed the pipe to his daughter; she passed it to George Clark, Sr. George Clark, Sr. passed the pipe to George Clark, Jr. George Clark, Jr. passed it to Jim Manasco; Jim passed the pipe to Terra Manasco. The pipe cannot be looked at as a source of pleasure; therefore, it will never be in a museum.

Ruth and Jim first lived in Birmingham across from Birmingham Southern College, but the call of the forest would eventually bring them back to their beloved Sipsey. Jim worked for Dixie Neon Sign Company. Jim stayed in the sign company business until 1961 and then started his own sign business; he worked on a percentage and got 60% with no expenses.

Jim and Ruth eventually started their move toward the land of their ancestors; they moved from Forestdale west of Birmingham into a new subdivision. In 1970, they made their home on Clear

Lower Clear Creek Falls

Creek of Smith Lake; the Manascos were finally in their homeland.

Jim fished Clear Creek when he was a little boy and Ruth grew up camping at Clear Creek Falls. Ruth's mother and their family would come to fish and lived under the bluff shelter at Clear Creek Falls. Nancy Pearl Estelle Sides married Arthur Lee Castleberry; Arthur and Pearl would bring their whole family to Clear Creek Falls to camp a few days; therefore, both Ruth and Jim had ties to Clear Creek.

Initially, Jim and Ruth lived in a house trailer on their

Smith Lake lot and eventually built an A frame cabin; Jim and two helpers built the A frame. Jim and Ruth sold the A frame and lot; they kept the lot where they now live and reconstructed an authentic Cherokee log cabin made from chestnut trees.

Today, Ruth and Jim live on Clear Creek in a log cabin that came from Qualla Boundary in Cherokee, North Carolina; Qualla Boundary is the Indian reservation of the federally recognized Eastern Band of Cherokees. Jim and Ruth's log cabin is about three miles upstream from the flooded Upper Clear Creek Falls; the falls are now some 30 feet under the backwaters of Smith Lake.

Ruth and Jim

Their Cherokee Indian made log home was built around 1900 for a federally recognized Eastern Cherokee man by the name of Sim Taylor; another Cherokee Indian was paid $50.00 to cut the chestnut timber, hang the logs, and make windows in the house. Sim Taylor's house was dismantled and transported on a flatbed Kenworth 18 wheeler truck to the Manasco's Smith Lake lot about 1985. Jim and his friends worked to put the log house back together; the numbered logs were picked out and put up over several years. The bathroom door of their Cherokee log cabin is off the old jail house that was located in Cherokee, North Carolina.

Both Jim and Ruth were originally members of the Cherokees of Northeast Alabama of the Chickamauga faction; they later became members of the Blue Clan of Echota Cherokee of Alabama that represent the Indian people of their homeland. Jim and Ruth Manasco's knowledge of the Bankhead Forest and Sipsey River drainage came from their Cherokee ancestors. In honor of their Cherokee ancestry, Jim and Ruth did Indian art shows over Southeastern United States for 15 years from 1990 until 2005.

Pine Tree Conversion

In the early 1960s, Jim and Ruth became advocates for wilderness preservation of the upper Sipsey River drainage in order to halt clear cutting in William B. Bankhead National Forest around the Bee Branch Scenic Area; Jim and Ruth were determined to stop the destruction of the old growth hardwoods and the conversion of the Sipsey to a pine tree farm. Bee Branch and the Big Tree would eventually become the central focus of their fight to save, protect, and preserve the area that became the Sipsey Wilderness.

The United States Forest Service had this brilliantly asinine idea that they could meet the needs of the paper industry by converting the Sipsey drainage area into big pine plantations with neat rows of loblolly pine trees. Therefore, instead of protecting the natural forest that Mother Nature had nurtured in the Black Warrior Mountains for eons of time, the forest service started a systematic destruction of the old growth hardwoods that dominated the Sipsey; during their bulldozing, road building, and clear cutting, the forest service converted over sixty percent of our native hardwood forest to commercial pine plantations.

Mother Nature did not surrender Sipsey without a fight; during a severe drought, the forest service was dealt a blow when thousands of acres of commercially planted

> Pine beetles were waiting on the forest service to feed their ravenous appetites. However, the forest service was unable to provide the beetles with enough pine food, but you have to give these forestry officials credit; they tried to fatten every pine beetle in North Alabama.

pure pine stands on the ridge tops of Bankhead died; the hot, dry summer was a violent slap in the face of the forest service and an obvious sight of gross mismanagement of the forest ecosystem. You could drive along the roads through the Sipsey drainage of the forest and see hundreds of acres of the skeletons of the dead loblolly pines. Within a short time, these dead pine plantations were being replaced by native hardwoods.

Mother Nature did not stop here; pine beetles were waiting on the forest service to feed their ravenous appetites. However, the forest service was unable to provide the beetles with enough pine food, but you have to give these forestry officials credit; they tried to fatten every pine beetle in North Alabama.

After the Sipsey Wilderness Area was established, Mother Nature did not take but a few years to destroy an area of a pure stand of some 40 acres of mature pines along the Thompson Creek Valley between White Oak Hollow and Hook Rock Shelter. Today, most of the huge pine logs that fell are now rotted and returned to the soil; this area has been reclaimed by

Mother Nature and returned to the native forest of the Black Warrior Mountains.

Fire Observation Towers

Pine tree conversion was as psycho genius of the United States Forest Service as the building of fire towers all across the William B. Bankhead National Forest in order to prevent devastating crown fires like those that occur in the western states; somebody never told the forest service managers that North Alabama did not have the same dry climate of the Rocky Mountain states, or maybe they forgot that hardwood trees shed their leaves in the fall. The forest service spent thousands of tax payer dollars building fire observation towers across Bankhead Forest before they finally figured out that our North Alabama climate was not as dry as Arizona.

During the summertime of the year in the Sipsey River drainage, the deciduous hardwoods trees and shrubs have green leaves that will not burn easily, while during the winter months these same trees have no leaves; therefore, the probability of a crown fire that could destroy a native forest in our area did not exist while it was in hardwoods. Surely, the forest service had long range plans of converting all our native hardwoods to commercial pine plantations a long time ago; with a pure pine forest, I am sure there would have been the need to have many fire observation towers.

Shortly after organizing the forest in the early 1920s and '30s, the United States Forest Service built several fire towers to protect the Sipsey River drainage from crown fires that would never happen in its deciduous hardwood forest. They built the following observation fire towers across the northern part of the forest in Lawrence County, Alabama: one was built just southeast of the junction of the Leola Road and Penn School Road at Basham; another just north of the junction of the Hickory Grove Road and the Leola Road, and west of the Flint Creek Road; the main tower just south of the junction of the Beech Creek Road and Cheatham Road (Sipsie Trail) called Central Tower; another tower just east of the junction of the Gum Pond Road and the Braziel Creek Road; and, one at David Hubbard's old home site at Kinlock.

In Franklin County, the forest service built another fire observation tower west of the Kinlock Road and Byler Road on the eastern edge of Franklin County just west of the Corral Rock Shelter. In Winston County, they built a fire tower east of the junction of the Hickory Grove Road and Sipsie Trail at Moreland in Winston County. In the Addison area and Black Pond area, the forest service had fire observation towers; there may have been many other fire towers that were built in Winston County.

It took several years for the professional experts in the United States Forest Service to realize that the fire observation towers were a waste of time and our money; if they would have been able to convert the whole forest into a big pine plantation, the towers may have been worth all the effort. Today you can see the fine example of this forest service fiasco at the Central Tower at the Black Warrior Work Center on Highway 33; with the exception of Central Tower, you can only find the concrete bases of the remnants of this bureaucratic waste of taxpayer money. Ask the United States Forest Service officials over the Bankhead Forest how many days and how much federal funds they waste with maintenance and observers in their remaining tower.

Now, the forest service does not worry about the fire observation towers unless they want to see the devastation of the fires

> With the exception of Central Tower, you can only find the concrete bases of the remnants of this bureaucratic waste of taxpayer money.

they deliberately set; each year, they used public funds and manpower to burn the forest they are supposed to protect. During the late winter, the forest service burns thousands of acres of leaf litter across Bankhead to prevent devastating wild fires that will never happen in this humid southeastern hardwood forest of Sipsey River; these fires kill all kinds of flora and fauna that are intolerant to the extreme heat.

Forestry officially ignores the warning of their own mascot Smokey the Bear, "*Only you can prevent forest fires!*" Today, you hear very little about Smokey the Bear because the forest service deliberately set fires that kill the majority of hardwood saplings and unknown numbers of organisms to promote the growth of pine trees which are somewhat fire resistant.

Sipsey Activists

At the same time Jim and Ruth were fighting for the wilderness, I, Rickey Butch Walker, became an activist against the clear cutting of Bankhead Forest. Starting in 1966, I would take posters made by two of my high schools teachers, Dennis Gilbreath and Warren Herron, and place them on trees and vehicles along the Bunyan Hill Road, Northwest Road, Gum Pond Road, and Braziel Creek Road. I would staple the cartoons making fun of the forest service's clear cutting activities on many of the trees around the Bee Branch Scenic Area.

In 1966, you could drive your vehicle to a parking area just above the Big Tree and walk down hill within a few minutes to view the majestic wonder of the State Champion Yellow Poplar that was situated in the east fork of Bee Branch Canyon. I well remember driving the road leading from the Bunyan Hill Road to the parking area on the hill just above the Big Tree; I also remember the first time I walked down hill to the tree and give it a big hug like everyone did to see just how big it really was. On my first visit in the early 1960s, it seemed as though no one ever climbed down that bluff into Bee Branch Canyon to see the Big Tree; the area around the tree was over grown with all kinds of understory vegetation and low herbaceous flowering plants. Today, you will not see an array of small plants around the tree; we are loving it to death.

During the days of gun deer hunts held on the Black Warrior Wildlife Management Area, Dennis Gilbreath would let me out on the Bunyan Hill Road with a stack of posters; I would place the cartoons under the wiper blades of the deer hunter's vehicles. Dennis Gilbreath and Warren Herron were teachers in Lawrence County Schools; they were mixed-blood Cherokee Indian descendants of the old forest families; they literally loved to turkey hunt and felt that clear cutting was not only destroying their cultural heritage but also their turkey hunting habitat. The two men spent hours making cartoons and posters; these posters were copied on the school mimeograph machines and I was anxious to place these posters in the forest.

During those early days of fighting for the wilderness, Jim and Ruth told me they collected some of the posters that I had put up against clear cutting. Mary Burks, who was the president of the Alabama Conservancy, and members of the group also collected some of the anti-clear cutting posters; Mary Burks later told John Randolph that she knew I put up many of the posters, but would not breathe a word to forestry officials for fear that I would be arrested.

The following are quotes from John M. Randolph in his 2005 book *The Battle for Alabama's Wilderness* found on pages 13 and 14: "*In northwest Alabama, Jim and Ruth Manasco were the most effective local advocates, as was one Rickey Butch Walker. Bob and Mary Burks tell of early Bankhead trips in which they encountered numerous hand-made signs posted around logged areas. She absconded with a few, which she showed me. One features an angry and cursing Smokey Bear, declaring, 'I QUIT (*@&*$*%@* Censored) The Forest Service is Doing More Damage Than Forest Fires.'*

Mary Ivy and Bob Burks

Another, titled 'Where Have All the Oak Trees Gone?' depicts a starving turkey and rabbit saying, respectively, 'I could never eat pine cones' and 'These pines just kill me.' A third shows deer, turkey, and squirrel gathered around a sign in front of a clear-cut that reads, 'This Area is Clearcut to be Planted in Pine Trees, All Wildlife is banned by order of the U.S. Forest Service.' Then 'What Do You Want—Wildlife or Pine Trees?'

Mary says, 'We were struck with admiration. The Forest Service said they were going to get the FBI to track down the people who were doing all this.' When Mary heard that Butch Walker was the culprit, she was afraid to mention it or discuss it, for fear she would be called to testify against him. The Forest Service never succeeded in their hunt for the sign maker, if they conducted such a search at all, and Butch Walker today remains a vocal Bankhead advocate and leader in the group known as Wild Alabama."

Along with Jim and Ruth Manasco and other wilderness advocates who were members of the Alabama Conservancy, Charles Borden and I, Rickey Butch Walker, teamed up to do our part on a local level to assist with the establishment and protection of the Sipsey Wilderness Area. Charles and I joined the Alabama Conservancy and became outspoken advocates to the wilderness preservation and stopping of clear cutting; we met with loggers, forestry officials, and the news media in adversarial situations.

On one occasion after meeting with loggers and officials, Charles and I were allowed to be the first group to take Clint Claybrook, a news writer, on a short trip; he was then to re-turn to Central Tower to interview the opposing views. We took him to the huge white oak stand just northeast of the Big Tree; by the time we got back to Central Tower, the loggers and officials had given up and left in disgust. This was bad judgment on our part because the article was very negative toward creating the Sipsey Wilderness Area; Charles Borden had a forest service employee attack him during the debate over the wilderness.

Even after the Sipsey Wilderness Area was designated, the clear cutting was continuing at an alarming rate. On August 22, 1991, I wrote an article to be published in the Moulton Advertiser in my Bankhead Back Trails section about clear cutting of Indian Tomb Hollow; after the article came out, a man knocked on my door and introduced himself as Lamar Marshall. Lamar was the godsend that would be instrumental in stopping clear cutting in William B. Bankhead National Forest; through his efforts and dedication, the mass destruction of our native hardwood forest slowed to a snail's pace.

After that meeting of Lamar and me, the Bankhead Monitor was started; that day, I paid the first year for our Post Office Box 114 at the Moulton Post Office. My former teacher Dennis Gilbreath gave me three full boxes of 11 inch by 17 inch Champion paper; at that time, Dennis was principal of Mount Hope High School and got free paper from Champion Paper Mill at Courtland, Alabama. It is ironic that on this free industrial commercial paper provided by Champion Paper Company the first Bankhead Monitor was published in Lawrence County, Alabama. The Bankhead Monitor was changed to Wild Alabama and then to Wild South; I was chairman of the Board of Directors until Wild South merged with the Southern Appalachian Biodiversity Project in 2006.

Jim and Ruth Manasco, Lamar Marshall, Charles Borden, and I became the best of friends; we had many things in common during our fight to preserve a part of our heritage and culture in the Sipsey Wilderness Area. During the time Lamar Marshall was director of Wild South, we got the United States Forest Service to provide protection to the Indian Tomb

Hollow, High Town Path, and the Kinlock Rock Shelter areas; these cultural heritage sites are considered Traditional Cultural Properties of those mixed-blood Celtic Indian descendants that live in North Alabama. These sacred aboriginal landscapes are found adjacent to the north and western boundaries of the present-day Sipsey Wilderness Area.

Many other people worked with Jim and Ruth during their fight for the wilderness area. These people were some of the most noted authorities in the State of Alabama and included the following: Thomas A. Imhof, Mike Hopiak, James Peavey, Mike Howell, Don Dyckus, Louise G. "Weese" Smith, Blanche Dean, Denny N. Bearce, Dale Carruthers, James and Fran Alexander, Charles Kelley, Ralph Allen, Dan Holliman, and Jim and Ruth Manasco.

Thomas A. Imhof of Birmingham and author of "Alabama Birds" was over ornithology, which was the study of birds. Mike Hopiak, a good friend of the Manascos, was from Birmingham and went to Cornell University. Mike worked with James Peavey in herpetology, which was the study of reptiles. Mike poured his knowledge and expertise into saving the wilderness of Sipsey. Dr. Mike Howell from Samford University and Don Dyckus with the Alabama Conservation were over ichthyology and did the fish study in the streams running through the Sipsey area in order to preserve the wilderness for all Alabamians.

Louise (Weese) Smith was a botanist, and she was the plant expert in Alabama. Weese worked with Blanche Dean in the botany of the area; Blanche was an author of fern and wildflower books on Alabama flora. Denny N. Bearce from Birmingham Southern University was over the geology. Dale Carruthers was over the history of the wilderness area. James and

Fran Alexander of the Huntsville Grotto of the National Speleological Society worked on the caves in Bankhead. Charles Kelley and Ralph Allen with the Alabama Game and Fish were over the wildlife. Dan Holliman with Birmingham Southern University was over the nongame wildlife.

Jim and Ruth's family worked on mapping the proposed Sipsey Wilderness Area; Jim Manasco provided descriptions of the wilderness and helped identify the original Sipsey Wilderness boundaries. Mary Burks was first president of Alabama Conservancy; she was a very effective political leader of the conservancy and worked with United States legislative delegations to get congressional approval of the Sipsey Wilderness Area. Mary was born on December 11, 1920, and died on February 16, 2007.

Jim and Ruth were dedicated to the purpose and cause of preserving the Sipsey Wilderness Area; they were charter members of Alabama Conservancy. Jim, Ruth, and their three children spent countless days of donated time without a thought of losing money. Most weeks Jim and Ruth's family would spend the weekends plus one work day each week camping and working on plants, birds, and history for the proposed Black Warrior Wilderness.

Ruth said, "*About 1965, we found a plant in the Bankhead National Forest that was so beautiful; it could have been an exotic plant from another country. Jim drew a detailed picture of the plant, and we took it to our librarian friend, Dolly Stack at the Pratt City Library. She said the plant was a hymenocallis lily. Dolly was a member of the Birmingham Audubon Society and was a wildflower photographer on her weekends and weekly off day. She took us to a Thursday night Audubon meeting where Blanche Evans Dean was giving the presentation that night on wildflowers.*

They had three or four live plants for show and I became familiar with my first trillium; I learned it had 3 petals, 3 sepals, and 3 leaves. Two days later Jim and I loaded the three kids up and went down to the Warrior River to Lock 17, and found the trillium plants. You talk about a discovery, it set us both on fire and we never looked back.

We spent the next few years visiting the Bankhead National Forest, including many field trips with the Birmingham Audubon Society. Some of our best memories are the field trips with Blanche Dean, author of 'Wildflowers of Alabama.' It was during this period that she was trying to get her book published; Jim and I put in our order for four books, one for each of the children and one for us. When it was published, she signed all of them. It was a joy to see how some people can grow older, without being old."

Jim Manasco Interview by Lamar Marshall

The following is an interview done with Jim Manasco in January 1999 by Lamar Marshall. The interview was recorded in the words of Jim and is as he spoke some ten years after the wilderness addition of 1989. Jim donated the original Sipsey Wilderness maps to Wild Alabama; the maps were the hand marked topos taken to Washington when the Sipsey Wilderness (later Eastern Wilderness Bill) was passed by Congress. The original map of Sipsey Wilderness Area that Jim Manasco took to Washington, D.C. was donated to the Alabama Department of Archives and History by Wild South.

Lamar: *Tell me how the Sipsey Wilderness started!*

Jim: *When we started this thing in 1970, we had a meeting in Montgomery with all the different conservation groups under* the blanket cover of the Alabama Conservancy. The decision was that they would have a concerted effort to establish a wilderness area east of the Mississippi River because there was not any east of the Mississippi River. And the specifications we had to work under were western wilderness. The big question was whether or not this wilderness here would qualify. I was

Lamar Marshall

asked at that meeting to co-chair the wilderness feasibly study with Dr. Charles Prigmore. That he would handle the political end and I would get the different scientific groups in and out of the proposed wilderness without getting lost and show them roughly where the perimeters would be for the study they were to make.

Over a period of five years, me and Ruth went with these groups into the forest and kept them inside the perimeter of what we thought would best qualify as wilderness. This map took five years to draw and we went to all of these areas and this had never been done beforehand. We really didn't have any guidelines to go by and we were trying to lessen the impact in describing the area so that it would not infringe on private properties or any of the other problems you would have in legislation to have it done.

What happened was that the area would not qualify as wilderness as was required in the wilderness act. The wilderness act said that it had to be road less and contain over 5,000 acres. So we just roughly drew a perimeter around this area and the Forest Service established a moratorium on the area by the roads: Kinlock Road, Cranal Road, and Bunyan Hill Road north to Northwest Road and around Northwest Road. Quite a few areas around this had already been clear-cut which disqualified it. The old logging roads disqualified it, but since most of those roads had been barricaded and were not in use we started drawing this map and over the years we were privileged to taking a lot of U.S. Congressmen, Senators, Postmaster General Blount, and quite a few dignitaries into the area. Over the years, we got to know them personally.

In the process, I started running a perimeter line cutting out quite a few tracts that the forest service had placed inside simply because they were so over cut and abused that they would not qualify. This is the final map here when they decided to go ahead and introduce it as special legislation to be a wilderness whether it qualified under the old specifications or not. The map showed where the wilderness would be; there were many people that did a lot of work before the Washington and Alabama delegation decided to introduce it in the House and Senate at the same time.

There was a question of where was the Sipsey Wilderness and I was called to come up there to Washington and meet with them to answer some questions as to where the wilderness was; I carried this map with me and the wilderness society had hooked me up with all the key people who were going to introduce the bill. I carried the map with me; set down in their congressional

43

offices. I was questioned pretty heavily about the area by Senator John Sparkman and again by Senator Jim Allen and Congressmen Buchanan and Tom Bevill. I told them basically why these sections were left out and that it was designed for minimum amount of impact on private property and accessibility and just a whole group of different reasons.

Throughout the entire study, this was to be the Black Warrior Wilderness Area. While I was in Washington, they were having some racial problems and somebody set off a bomb in the Senate restroom. And the next morning they came to me and said they needed a new name really fast and that it was not good to introduce a bill with the name of Black Warrior on it and that they needed a different name. The only name I could come up with at the time was the Sipsey Wilderness; that is why it is named the Sipsey.

This was a very involved process; before I left, I carried the map to Tom Bevel who carried it to the U.S. Forest Service and asked them to define the boundaries for the bill that was to be introduced. The forest service did a good job of defining the map, but there were three things I had in my description that they left out. One of those was Johnson Cemetery; the boundary of Johnson Cemetery was to go down one side of the access road to the cemetery and around the cemetery and back up the other side of the road and leave the access and the cemetery out of the wilderness area. They were to do the same thing at Wolf Pen Cemetery and the knob on the north side of Cranal Road at Sipsey Recreation Area it was supposed to have followed the old Cranal Road and cut out a tract of land on the top of the hill to be used in the future as a nature interpretive center and a parking lot. But these three things they left out so I don't know if these things are in the wilderness or not because they are left

44

out of the description the forest service gave but not in the description I gave to Tom Bevill.

Something else that was going on at the time was a lot of conflict between the forest service and other people that were trying to establish wildernesses in other national forests east of the Mississippi River. They came to me and said knowing my personality that I was going to be unhappy about what was going to happen on the floor of the Senate and the House and told me what was fixing to occur. They were having hearings and over a hundred people were to testify before the Senate Affairs Committee on why there were no wildernesses east of the Mississippi River. At the same time this was going on and they explained to me that this bill on the Sipsey Wilderness was to be introduced and immediately pulled off the floor and that the whole bill would then be reintroduced to include all of those other wilderness areas east of the Mississippi River.

They would be adding the other areas and the name would be changed to the Eastern Wilderness Bill including all of the other all the others that now exist east of the Mississippi River. The Forest Service was to go back under Rare II mandate to look at other areas surrounding these wildernesses (RARE stands for Road less Areas Reevaluation). This Reevaluation that came out of these hearings was what doubled the size of the Sipsey Wilderness Area; Rare II added considerable more to the other wilderness areas too. This only happened here recently but I wanted you all to have this map because it is the birth place of all wildernesses east of the Mississippi River.

I guess the historical value of this map is too much for me to leave lying in a desk drawer somewhere; so y'all can have it to display here. If for any reason you see fit that it should go somewhere else, I would recommend either the Moundville Museum or the Lawrence County Library. I'm not putting any restrictions of any kind on this map; I just want to know that it is in a safe place.

Lamar: *What are the Areas?*

Jim: *Okay, according to what I had written, I broke it up into areas.*

Area 1, *because of its accessibility to the Recreation area and possibly a future Nature Interpretive center, was to be heavily used; you know it concentrated people.*

Area 2 *is pretty much cut over and not very scenic, but it was necessary as a buffer to get the amount of space we needed trying to make it qualify under too stringent requirements.*

Area 3 *is Bee Branch which would be mostly trails and wilderness experience area.*

Area 4 *is the most unusual historic, scenic, and everything else of all of the wilderness area. I had recommended that area four not have any trails or anything that would cause it to environmentally deteriorate. In this area you have Kinlock Falls, which is heavily used. The Kinlock Antiquities Area should have been inside the wilderness but the requirements said that the boundary could not cross a road so they were left out. As it goes around the outside boundary, these little squares were privately owned tracts where I am cutting out as much privately owned land as possible. There were only two forty-acre tracts left inside and the forest service has agreed that they would trade other lands for those. This was economics not having to raise money to buy 80 acres that was all of the privately owned land inside that whole perimeter that could be traded off. That was a key thing because it took no financing to do this only a proclamation more or less. In order to get the canyon on Borden Creek and all,*

I defined it by the 500 foot escarpment or 500 foot elevation line; this is now inside the wilderness.

Lamar: *You need to write on the bottom of this map that you carried to Tom Bevill and to congressmen in Washington D.C. Sign your name Jim Manasco; fifty or a hundred years from now that map will be a treasure. It will be in the Lawrence County Archives or the Winston County Archives or the Moundville Museum.*

Jim: *Something else that happened that is very significant and was bringing a lot of comments in, I just do not really know what the outcome will be. Because of so many people working on this project were elderly and handicapped, it just did not seem fair that they should be denied access to wilderness. So in the process, the Northwest Road was to remain open so that they could have easy access to see that beautiful scenery and all that along the road. When the forest service described this area, they set the boundary of the wilderness area 66 feet from the center of the road. So half of the road way of the Northwest Road going through the forest now is 66 feet to the wilderness; I would assume that when they added the addition to the wilderness, they added another 66 feet on the other side of the road as boundaries between the two wildernesses and the Northwest Road was not to be inside the wilderness area. There would have been an easement 132 feet wide all across the wilderness for handicapped access; oddly enough the first thing the forest service did was close Northwest Road, which in effect denied handicapped people that access.*

At the time, I had no idea that it would be as heavily used as it is and I do not know now whether or not the Northwest Road should be reopened; however, a person can still drive a wagon through it. Well this is a forest service regulation that has nothing to do with the wilderness legislation; this is just a restriction they put on it themselves, the forest service did that and it has nothing to do with the Eastern Wilderness Bill.

Because that quarter is still there, I protested it being set back 66 feet, but it was done anyway because of the threat of falling trees. What this does is set the wilderness signs so far back off of the road that people looking for the wilderness boundary cannot find it. This was done at a time when visual resource management was a major part of clear cutting; you left a strip of trees along the road so that you could not see the ugly clear cuts from the road; they won this set back from the road as part of visual resource management; that is what they were calling it at the time. This gave them the authority to cut and do anything they wanted for 66 feet between the road and the actual wilderness boundary where there would not be that sudden change from what management looks like to what wilderness looks like. Because of the embarrassment that would be associated with it, so that is why there is such a tremendous right of way on those roads.

Lamar: *What do the triangles mean?*

Jim: *Those are waterfalls; they are not all on the map, I was just recording the ones that were unusual.*

Lamar: *Who was the first person to say, "Why don't we make the Bee Branch area a wilderness?"*

Jim: *Charles Prigmore was a lobbyist at the University of Alabama. There were several of those guys who got together; one* was Joe Ab Thomas from the University; another one was Denny Bearce from University of Alabama at Birmingham. Oddly enough after it started, Charlie just disappeared.

Lamar: *Who was Mary Burks?*

Jim: *Mary Burks was the president of the Alabama Conservancy. She was not the coordinator of the wilderness, but she is considered the Grandmother of the Bankhead's wilderness. Mary worked really hard; she did a lot of good. She was one of the really hard workers and devoted five years of her life to nothing but saving the wilderness in Bankhead Forest; she was not alone.*

There were others doing the same: Dan Holliman was from Birmingham Southern; Walter Cox was a bird man from the Alabama Ecological Society; Mike Hopiak represented the Southeastern Ecological Society; Blanche Dean had this dream all her life and wanted to see a nature interpretive center in the Bankhead National Forest; Mike Howell was the ecologist and fish man; Bob Mount from Auburn University was dealing with reptiles; and, the group included the Audubon Society and all sorts of people from the Sierra Club.

I have it written down somewhere and there were so many, but one year there were 75 days of carrying groups to the area who were from different colleges and universities. Probably the widest reaching would be Dr. Aldo Braco from Argentina. He and his wife had come; they used to visit me and spent a lot of time up here studying. He went back to Argentina and established a reserve there because of what he had seen here; it was massive.

I was just overwhelmed by the reception I got from Washington. I was assigned a page; I was carried around to all these people who are very prominent. A page would get me to all these people who we were seeing; I walked in every door of all the senators and congressmen; everybody was setting there ready to talk to me. I was just ushered in and I was carried all through the capital to all these other people; now, it was an experience.

Lamar: *What did you tell them?*

Jim: *They wanted to know where the wilderness was and they were just asking me questions concerning where the boundaries were and why this was cut out. The bill they had drawn up said that the boundaries would be defined at a later date until Ernie Dickerson of the Wilderness Society had learned that I had already drawn them out; this is why they wanted me up there. They figured one person with the map could do it quicker than a lot of people without a map. So basically just the map is what they wanted described.*

Lamar: *The areas in the wilderness that were clear cut are restoring so fast.*

Jim: *It will, I am really surprised at Thompson Creek; it has changed totally. I cannot account for how all of those plants that were so rare when we were doing this survey that same trail now by Borden Creek could come back with such lush patches. I don't know why unless the buffer around it somehow helped to put the ecosystem back together. I have always felt that converting these ridge tops from hardwood to pine was going to make a big difference in what is in the valleys because of the acid runoff. Its changing the water that is going down into these big patches of Goldenseal, Waterleaves, and Dutchmen's Britches; stuff that you would expect to go to the Smokies to even see, have come back now in lush patches.*

I think it is because the pines are dying out because of the beetles. The pines are dying out and its going back to hardwood drainage. I have been in this forest now for 65 years and I have seen it change from wilderness to timber production and now it is going back to wilderness again. It is surprising just what a buffer zone can impact, how much effect it really has. They have realized this on scenic rivers; if you really want to kill a river, just cut the trees down around the banks. I did not know it would work in this big of an area.

A long time ago you and I talked about hemlocks and how old they were; Bee Branch Canyon has the biggest hemlock you have ever seen. If you came off of Northwest Road and went down to the Big Tree where you go down the embankment to get to the Big Tree, you started walking right at the foot of the escarpment on your left and just followed it around. You will come to a little trail that goes up in a break in the bluff, go on by that little trail and keep following the eastern side of the escarpment. You will walk right to a huge hemlock. It is right in the edge of the escarpment. It is in Bee Branch not far from the Big Tree.

That big tree is probably the biggest yellow poplar tree in the World. I went to the biggest poplar tree recorded in the Smoky Mountains and that tree puts it to shame yellow poplars in Joyce-Kilmer. Some people don't realize that in the canyon just across from the Big Tree is full of huge poplars, almost

Blanche Evans Dean
6/12/1892-5/31/1974

52

as big as the big tree. There were a lot of them around the area; I would tell people who wanted to see these to walk on past the trail into Bee Branch and just straight on down the old logging road till they heard the frogs sing, and then turn left. Because there is big spring up on the top of that ridge that makes a wet area and it is always full of frogs. When you get to that pond, you can hear the frogs before you get to it up on that ridge; you never hear a frog up on a ridge. Now there is a series of five waterfalls that you can zigzag down to, just follow the runoff from that spring and you will go right down into those big poplars. This is the only way you can get in; coming down the ridge here to where the trees are.

If you went down the old low back to Johnson Cemetery and went all the way to the old rock cabin, you will find an old horse trail that goes down the bluff, it's grown up. That is a stand of yellow magnolias that you walk under. But they are so tall and skinny that you do not know it. Just before the leaves come on the trees, those trees will bloom and all the yellow blooms will be laying everywhere.

The most unusual plant expert is Louise (Weese) Smith, probably Alabama's greatest botanist. Academically she is above Blanche Evans Dean, but Blanche Dean had that old timey naturalist in her. Instead of talking about Latin names, and related species and all that like Weese tends to, she would be telling you about what the pioneers used these plants for and what the old timers thought about them. This kind of stuff Blanche just had that reach out and touch people, and two of the people she touched the most are Weese Smith and Mary Burks. If it hadn't been for Blanche Dean, they would have never seen the Bankhead I guess. Well, they would have eventually come to it, but not as soon.

I had no idea it would be so heavily used; I haven't been in there lately, but I understand that is has just been really trampled. But I was faced with this; the forest service had planned to clear cut the whole wilderness, ridge tops, canyons, and all. At the time of the moratorium, they were constructing a road down the ridge next to Bee Branch. The forest service had gone all the way through to access this in order to clear cut; they were going to plant all the ridges in pine and the canyons in poplar; only two species. The forest service would have completely destroyed the entire wilderness.

I spent my whole life in that cabin right down there on Caney Creek and I have spent my whole life in here and did not want to see people, it was sort of a selfish thing, I just didn't want to see a lot of people, it was my place. And I could go in there and never see anybody. Then when I learned what was fixing to happen here, I had my choice I could either see it all destroyed or share it with a lot of people. I chose to share it rather than lose it, and that is how I became involved. I just could not see the best piece of Alabama be sent to a chipper and that is what was going to happen to it.

Lamar: We have the wilderness expansion now and we are faced with a decision. The plan revision is going on; they have four themes. One of them is to cut the whole thing down except the wilderness. Another is to leave the forest alone. Another says to restore the forest. And the last says, we would like to make the northern one third of the Bankhead-from the Leola Road north, taking in the Kinlock Historic District, all the way down to Grayson, and all of the northern Bankhead-and make it a National Recreation Area. It could be written in there to have no commercial logging and no over development of recreation. What do you think about that?

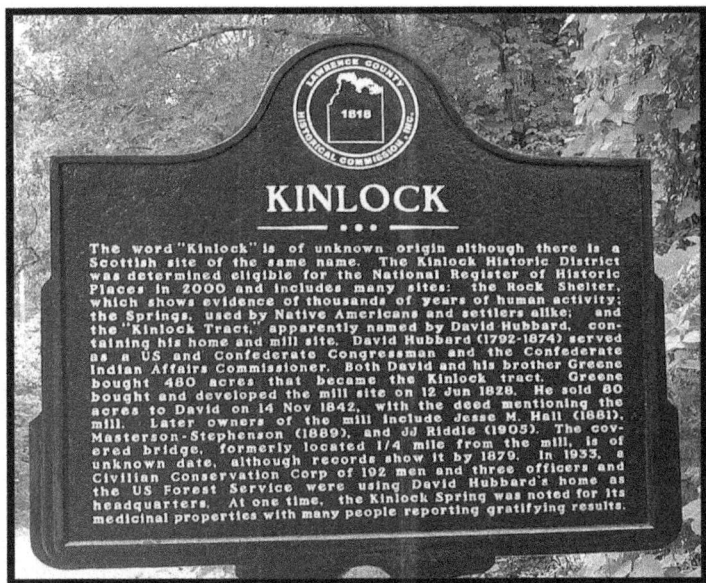

KINLOCK
• • •

The word "Kinlock" is of unknown origin although there is a Scottish site of the same name. The Kinlock Historic District was determined eligible for the National Register of Historic Places in 2000 and includes many sites: the Rock Shelter, which shows evidence of thousands of years of human activity; the Springs, used by Native Americans and settlers alike; and the "Kinlock Tract," apparently named by David Hubbard, containing his home and mill site. David Hubbard (1792-1874) served as a US and Confederate Congressman and the Confederate Indian Affairs Commissioner. Both David and his brother Greene bought 480 acres that became the Kinlock tract. Greene bought and developed the mill site on 12 Jun 1828. He sold 80 acres to David on 14 Nov 1842, with the deed mentioning the mill. Later owners of the mill include Jesse M. Hall (1881), Masterson-Stephenson (1889), and JJ Riddle (1905). The covered bridge, formerly located 1/4 mile from the mill, is of unknown date, although records show it by 1879. In 1933, a Civilian Conservation Corp of 192 men and three officers and the US Forest Service were using David Hubbard's home as headquarters. At one time, the Kinlock Spring was noted for its medicinal properties with many people reporting gratifying results.

Jim: *The forest service is not in charge, no matter what they tell you they are not in charge. The sole function of the U.S. Forest Service is to fulfill the requirements of the Congress of the United States. They will do whatever Congress tells them to do. Right now sitting here looking at this map all it would take is a presidential proclamation to change the whole Bankhead National Forest into a National Recreation Area; simply with the signature of the President. You don't have to have all of these studies; you don't have to have all of this work; it is pressure from the people; and it is the pressure from congress that makes forest service change their policies.*

I find it highly amusing, that after I got over the initial shock of carrying all this up there and doing this work for the wilderness, that thanks to Mary Burks and a lot of other people, especially Southern Living magazine, I was being sent to Washington with a petition that had over 350,000 signatures. It was not knowledge either by congress or environmental knowledge, or any of the bureaucracies like the forest service that did this, it was the 350,000 signatures. The voice of politics; politics can do anything politics wants to do. When those 350,000 people, many of them individuals and some signing in groups like the Sierra Club, 350,000 votes can get you elected president. This is something you don't mess with.

What you have done with your magazine here, is what brought all these people in here and every foot print in there; there are a 100 more people out there that would say the same thing. This is so much in the public eye the forest service has no choice, the State of Alabama has no choice; they have got to honor the historic preservation right; they have got to honor the endangered species act; they have got to honor the wilderness act.

There is a list two pages long of laws by congress not to regulate people, but to regulate the U.S. Forest Service. Just getting your story out; its education, it all boils down to education. When we started this, the Wilderness Society had only been in effect for five years. Historic preservation had only been in effect for one year. The vast majority of these people did not know all these laws had been passed. People just didn't know. And we were running blind. We did not know. We had to go back and look all over but we did have rights. Even people today think they don't but they do and lots of them.

When we did this, there was no such thing as surface mining, it was striping. There was no wilderness period; there was a silent spring. All of this is in the past; it is the 21st century. These kids in school are not environmentally ignorant like people were when we started the fight for wilderness.

I remember when we had a kangaroo court that put us all in jail for talking ugly about the forest service. We appealed it to

Bill Campbell at the college over there; we were all subpoenaed and asked to go home. The forestry association had their recorder hidden in the back room and I accidentally found it back there recording everything. The first thing we asked the kangaroo court people was that the recorder be left running. That we did not want it turned off. One of the major people protesting was slamming his fist and carrying on, real rude like. He says if we give you this what else are you going to want? I asked him to show me his deed. That it was my understanding that this already belonged to us.

Dr. Robert Mount got up and he said that I know you all say that we are just emotional, that we are working solely on emotions. He says that is true, when I see you all destroying everything I hold dear, I have every reason to become emotional. Auburn University really got deeply involved in this, simply because of people like him.

The wilderness has been really good for people in Winston County. The people that opposed it were those that were in logging and folks that were in charge of logging; however, there were many, many loggers that supported us. They said what they were doing was wrong, but they had no power to stop it; if they didn't cut the trees, the forest service would just get somebody else to do it. I don't know a single logger that opposed this thing. The Lawrence County Coon Hunters Association was a big supporter. It was across the board with the people of this area.

Those that said we would kill Double Springs by doing this, by taking out their livelihood, as soon as the bill was passed they turned 360 degrees. Because they found out what Alaska found out, that if you sell a tree for one dollar, people will pay two dollars to come see it if you do not cut it down.

This is what brought you here, what got you here now. If it had been left in the hands of the timber industry this place would not exist. You would not be here in this building. Tourism is the most lucrative and economic business in the world. "Double Springs is the gateway to the Sipsey Wilderness;" yeah, it wasn't at the time.

Let me tell you something, Neal Shipman, if you called him right now, would say, "I would like to apologize, what you said about wilderness was true." Of course, I was sort of dreaming because I didn't know it would be true, only assumed that it would be. Here lately, I have sat and thought about, since I was looking at this map, basically the same thing you asked me, if I could single out the one person that probably had a bigger influence on this than anybody else, would be Winton Blount. He called me and asked me to take him deep into the woods and I did. I took him down Johnson Cemetery Road, all the way to the cabin; we walked a log across Sipsey, and I carried him all the way to Bee Branch in his dress clothes. A whole entourage of Secret Service men followed because he was the Post Master General of the United States; he was a very powerful man. I didn't know that at the time; I treated them all pretty much the same.

We were setting on a log on the ridge along with the girl he brought with him. The Secret Service did not want him to walk back; the six or seven miles I had carried him back in the woods. Most of the people that were with us were afraid we were totally lost. Rayford Hyatt radioed for someone to come to Northwest Road to pick them up so that they could go back and get the cars. After getting ready to get him back out of there, we sat there I guess and hour or so and he turned to her and says do you hear that? She sat there and she says I do not hear anything. He turned to her and said, 'Do you realize how few places on the face on this earth you can go and not hear anything' and that was about how it was.

Later, I found out that Marl Hunt, up until 1985, was the number one influential and financial philanthropist and humanitarian that the states had ever produced. He had donated more money to the Hearts of Humanities than any other single person. Because of his association with wilderness, nobody seems to know just what a humanitarian he is. But going back and trying to see where all of this power was coming from; nobody has ever said thank you. Very few of the people that did all this work ever knew that he cared. He was just not that kind of person. I forget how many millions of dollars he has given to the Hearts of Humanities. Where did he make his money? I do not know. The thing that touches me most about him is, he has done more to give back the wilderness than his ancestors. If you look back at his grand dad, he has given back so much more to Indians and everybody else; then I would say that the debt was paid in full.

I would like to see that Kinlock be recognized as the birth place of the pony express; it is also the birth place of the U.S. Postal Service. With the Louisiana Purchase, the old Mobile Trace was the dispatch route went from Washington to St. Stephens which was the thick wilderness of the Louisiana Purchase. The dispatches that were sent back and forth were carried on horses which as a pony express. Sending expresses to Washington went through the ditch there at Kinlock. That was in 1804 and in 1818 the U.S. Postal Service was established and before that it was volunteer. People like William Tearis and people along here were volunteering; give the man a horse to carry it to the next place and doing the same thing coming back. The Government wasn't financing any of that; it was all volunteer. This is the pony express; it would be sixteen years later that the Government would establish pay for those riders who carried the expresses. Then in 1819 when Alabama became a state, the Byler Road was the first contracted road, the same road passing Kinlock, to improve mail service from Washington to St. Stephens. Kinlock is the birth place of the Pony Express and the U.S. Postal Service.

Since Winton Blount did such a fine job supporting this and he was the Postmaster General, there definitely should be a National Monument. While we sat there talking I had no idea that he even existed. I did not know until I started mapping that an after that, gosh that was 25 years ago. I knew where the old path was, but I did not know that it was the old dispatch route. We have just lost an endless amount of history. Simply because it has never been published. All of that information is in the state archives, where I found out that two people over in Mississippi.

You get this feeling that the forest service is trying to do this or trying to do that when actually we are suffering from the same thing. The forest service has no reason to know either of the historic value of Kinlock. I did but it was Native American and just local very local. I had no idea that it was a prominent in American history as it is. Of course, the High Town Path, that portion of it from Mt. Hope to Kinlock should bear the name the Mobile Trace because it was the main path from the great lakes to Tuscaloosa and it dead ended at Mobile. That is why it was called Mobile Trace; Mobile was the end of the loop, and from Mobile, you went by water.

The state put High Town Path signs all the way over to Mississippi; they are all across the state. The signs were posted at every major intersection of the High Town Path in Alabama and every county except this county here. They wouldn't pay for it, but I am sure the forest service would or the Department of the Interior. The Department of the Interior has a deep interest in the Bankhead Forest because half of the Bankhead National Forest belongs to the Department of the Interior. It is not owned *through the Forest Service. It was bought under the Wings Act which was brought to the Department of the Interior and placed in the corner of the U.S. Forest Service.*

Lamar: *I want to put Rayford Hyatt in the Magazine; he helped me in historic interest alone.*

Jim: *Rayford was in a peculiar position, the U.S. Forest Service appropriated no money for wildlife management in Bankhead Forest. It was left entirely to the state and Rayford was the only conservation officer in the Bankhead Forest; he did a good job. A lot of people thought he was hard, but he had to be because he was only one man covering an area as big as he did; he had to be hard. He loved the wilderness more than any man ever did; he helped everybody that came in here working on it. If you got stuck, if you got lost, Rayford was the man who got you out; he rescued a bunch of them. He would find out what they were looking for; what he did, he did quietly because he could not jeopardize what little conservation there was. He lost because the Forest Service had the ability to shut down the State of Alabama anytime they wanted to.*

The first conservation officer was Amos Spillers; he was a half- breed Cherokee, and he trained his replacement who was George Whitman. George Whitman was one quarter Cherokee; his mother was a Manasco. George was my second cousin; George trained Rayford Hyatt who was his replacement. There has only been three conservation officers since this forest was established. I knew George quite well; I never knew Amos Spillers. George was more by the book law than Rayford was; people just thought Rayford was tough because they never met George. Rayford had a sour side to him, and he had a real good since of humor.

61

Of all the experiences, I have had many in this forest, but one of my first experiences in tracking was how to track Rayford Hyatt. All my kinfolk have been in here all their lives; they did not hunt and fish by the book. When he would come through and asked questions and then go on, they would take me to where Rayford had been and make me look at his footprints and make me look at his cigarette butts. My folks made me look at the tires on his car; then they would take me out in the woods with them and make me find where he had been going before. They showed me where he would go down ridges; he would leave his car and walk. Rayford walked a lot; he would walk down these old log roads. My people would have me walk where he walked and walk in his tracks; where he would stop, I would have to stop and stand with my feet in his tracks so that I would be looking at whatever he was looking at. I could find where he would sit; we called it, squat on his haunches and stay for a long while and smoke two or three cigarettes. My kin would have me tell them what he was doing; when he would do that, it would be because he was listening. I thought it was just them trying to protect themselves because they were notorious for putting out fish traps, baiting deer and turkey, and everything else like that so they had to watch him real close.

Over the years, I came to know Rayford quite well; I guess I have respect for Rayford. One of the strangest things that I guess any conservation officer has ever done. He lived out there at Turkey Creek and his oldest son had gone fishing and I think the limit was 20 bass and he caught I think sixty and loaded up and took them back to the house. Him and Rayford sat there and cleaned them and there was 20 more fish there. Rayford pulled out his little citation book and wrote his son a ticket for catching over the limit. Then took the ticket up to the court house here in

Lawrence County and paid the fine. I asked Rayford, "Rayford why did you do that?" And he told me "He says it is not fair for me to go out there and write someone else's kid a ticket and not my own son." This has probably never happened before and will probably never happen again. But that tells you right there really what kind of a person Rayford Hyatt really was.

EASTERN WILDERNESS ACT OF 1975

Jim, Ruth, and their children were instrumental in getting the Sipsey Wilderness Area of William B. Bankhead National Forest preserved for future generations to enjoy; without compensation, the Manascos spend days, weeks, months, and years seeking the protection of an area they had learned to love from their parents and grandparents. It was this love and their dedication that helped to make the Sipsey Wilderness Area a reality for all people.

United States Postmaster General Winton Blount

Jim and Ruth guided the United States Postmaster General Winton Blount to Needles Eye and Ship Rock near the beginning of Sipsey River at the mouths of Thompson Creek and Hubbard Creek in Bankhead Forest. Jim said, "*Blount was surrounded by secret service and arrived in the forest in two black limos.*"

Winton Malcolm (Red) Blount was born in Union Springs, Alabama, on February 1, 1921, and died on October 24, 2002; he was Postmaster General when the position was a presidential cabinet member. In 1972, Republican Blount made an unsuccessful run against Democratic Senator John Sparkman; Blount carried Winston County, which contained a large portion of the proposed wilderness; however, both Alabama political leaders supported the creation of the Sipsey Wilderness.

United States Senator John Sparkman

United States Senator John Sparkman hiked to the Big Poplar with Jim and Ruth, who took a picnic lunch. Senator John Sparkman introduced the Eastern Wilderness Act of 1975; he was the most important political figure in the United States Congress to support the formation of the Sipsey Wilderness Area.

United States Senator John Jackson Sparkman was originally a United States Congressman in the House of Representatives before becoming a Senator; he was born on a North Alabama family farm near Hartselle, Alabama, in Morgan County. Sparkman was born on December 20, 1899, and died in Huntsville on November 16, 1985; he is interned in the Maple Hill Cemetery in Huntsville, Alabama.

Senator Sparkman worked hard to preserve an eastern wilderness for future generations in a portion of his homeland in the nearby William B. Bankhead National Forest located in the Black Warrior Mountains of Lawrence and Winston Counties, Alabama. Not only did his congressional act create the Sipsey Wilderness Area, but also included the first series of wilderness areas across the eastern portion of the United States.

Under the leadership of Senator John Sparkman, folks in North Alabama did the impossible! The people from North Alabama may not be the smartest of the species but intelligence has never been a match for dogged determination.

> **The people from North Alabama may not be the smartest of the species but intelligence has never been a match for dogged determination.**

What stirred them up was the

United States Forest Service cutting the native hardwoods down and then replanting nothing but pines. This mismanagement of the forest left it looking like a shredded wheat factory. No matter what was said the Forest Service would not

Senator John J. Sparkman

change its management plan. This left only one way to stop them, take it away from them, make it a wilderness, and then it would never be touched again.

Alabama was not alone; most every state east of the Mississippi was and still is having their national forests clear cut. Many had tried to have the best remaining portions of their forest saved under the 1964 Wilderness Act and had failed. The bill was so rigid that no land east of the Big River would qualify; of course, the Big River is what some folks call the Mississippi River. People had tried to save special areas as wilderness and failed.

The people of Alabama found that the Sipsey Wilderness would not qualify under the 1964 Act either. Not knowing any better, they determined that they should change the act to fit the forest.

They cried for help and it came. First as technical people doing the ground work for free; then followed by groups

> **Never get a redneck mad, you never know what they might do.**

formed of the strangest assortment this state has ever seen. Coon hunters helping bird watchers, national riflemen aiding wild flower people, little old women in tennis shoes leading boy scouts, pulpwood haulers helping historians with names of places and things, and would you believe, an abundant supply of foresters and forest service personnel working undercover so their employers would not know they were assisting. Never get a redneck mad, you never know what they might do. These local people changed the law with the Sipsey Wilderness Bill.

United States Senate Speech of John Sparkman

The following is the address made by the Honorable John Sparkman of Hartselle, Alabama, to the United States Senate as he introduced the bill proposing the Sipsey Wilderness Area:

It is with great pride and pleasure that I rise to introduce a bill which will assure permanently to the people of Alabama and of the nation the use and enjoyment of one of Alabama's splendid natural treasures, the proposed Sipsey Wilderness on the Bankhead National Forest situated in Lawrence and Winston Counties in northwest Alabama.

For generations the folks living in Northern Alabama have been going to the headwaters of the Sipsey River to enjoy the wild beauty of this area and to refresh themselves by roaming, camping, fishing, hunting and learning the ways of nature in this extraordinary piece of God's handiwork.

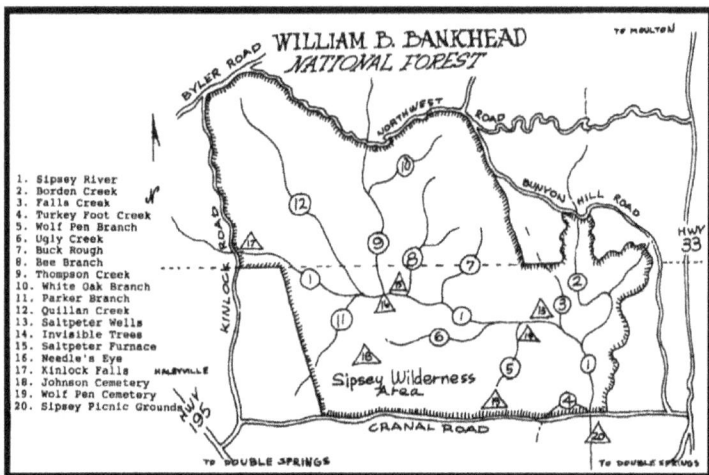

My bill would place approximately 12,000 acres of the headwaters of the Sipsey River in the National Wilderness Preservation System under the terms of the Wilderness Act of 1964. The protection provided by the Wilderness Act would guarantee by the surest means that the natural treasures within the proposed Sipsey Wilderness in the way of wildlife, plants, geology and rugged stream canyons will flourish and continue to be available for all people to see and know, to enjoy and understand.

The natural qualities of this forest and in particular of the proposed Sipsey Wilderness are remarkable because here the three major land masses or types east of the Rocky Mountains meet and overlap. This makes possible an extraordinary diversity of plants and animals in this area. This immensely varied combination of soils, water and climate provides a total environment which offers the essential living conditions for a range of life far in excess of that found almost anywhere else in the eastern United States. Its extraordinary combination of conditions and of life constitutes an area which demands preservation.

Geology has provided a naturally protected system on this part of the Bankhead Forest. The canyons are rimmed by massive bluffs of sandstone which form precipitous cliffs, some over 100 feet high. The canyons themselves are deep, shadowy and cool. Fossils from the late Paleozoic Era are abundant.

The proposed wilderness area is a veritable botanists' paradise. The cool, moist canyons provide suitable habitat for an essentially Appalachian flora but with unusual inclusions from the Piedmont to the east and Ozarkian area to the west. Cool summer temperatures in the gorges allow many plants to reach their southern geographical limit on the Bankhead. Two very rare and demanding representatives of the filmy-fern family are abundant in the proposed wilderness area. The lovely large Yellow Lady slipper, a native orchid of great beauty, is found amongst a carpet of rare and unusual mountain wildflowers growing unexpectedly far south. Two wild camellias, aristocrats of our native flowering shrubs, three species of deciduous magnolias, and Alabama's largest specimen of the tulip poplar are to be seen here. Large, vigorous hemlocks are especially noteworthy, as this is the southernmost range of the species.

Much is to be learned about the distribution and ecology of non-game mammals living in the proposed wilderness. Twenty-five of 53 species and subspecies of Southeastern mammals have been definitely recorded in the proposed wilderness tract. It appears probable that careful scientific study will disclose more species; such studies are currently under way. This area has been renowned for its abundance of game species of wildlife since Indian times. 147 species of birds are known to occur in the area including a substantial number which are largely dependent for

*their continued existence on woodland as it prevails in the pro-
posed wilderness area. Two species of amphibians (the barking
tree frog and the seal salamander) which were completely unexpected live here far from their previously known ranges.*

*In short, the fauna and flora of this area are unique and
attract great interest on the part of both scientists and ordinary
visitors alike. Such a wealth of living natural wonders cries out
for the full protection which can be provided through designating
this region as wilderness.*

*I submit for the consideration of this distinguished body my
bill to establish the Sipsey Wilderness and the Bankhead National Forest in Alabama. Future generations of Alabamians and
other Americans from all over the nation will enjoy the refresh-
ing and stimulating wilderness experiences to be gained here.
I urge you to consider the merits of this proposal and to lend
your support to the protection of this great natural wonder in the
State of Alabama.*

Other Wilderness Areas Saved

This was as far as the Sipsey Wilderness bill progressed; others
who had tried and failed to save their wilderness areas asked
the Alabama Congressional Delegation to withdraw the bill
and reintroduce it as the Eastern Wilderness Act, Public Law
93622 and add their areas to it; so it was done.

Alabamians saved their 12,000 acres in the William B.
Bankhead National Forest, but few realize that Alabamians
also helped save the following eastern wilderness areas: Caney
Creek Wilderness Area, Arkansas, 14,432 acres; Upper Buffalo
Wilderness Area, Arkansas, 10,590 acres; Bradwell Bay Wil-
derness Area, Florida, 22,000 acres; Beaver Creek Wilderness
Area, Kentucky, 5,500 acres; Presidential Range Dry River

Wilderness, 20,380 acres; Joyce Kilmer-Slickrock Wilderness Area, in North Carolina and Tennessee, 15,000 acres; Elliott Rock Wilderness Area, North and South Carolina and Georgia, 3,600 acres; Gee Creek Wilderness Area, Tennessee, 2,570 acres; Bristol Cliffs Wilderness Area, Vermont, 6,500 acres; Lye Brook Wilderness Area, Vermont, 14,300 acres; James River Face Wilderness Area, Virginia, 8,800 acres; Dolly Sods Wilderness Area, West Virginia, 10,250 acres; Otter Creek Wilderness Area, West Virginia, 20,000 acres, Rainbow Lake Wilderness Area, Wisconsin, 60,600 acres; Cohutta Wilderness Area, Georgia and Tennessee, 34,600 acres.

The Eastern Wilderness Act of 1975 also paved the way for further acceptance of other areas in other eastern states. In nine of these states, other wilderness areas increased the eastern wilderness by another 150,000 acres. Intelligence is no match for dogged determination, but what it took to save the wild lands was courage. Courage to go against all odds and that is what Alabamians do best.

> **Intelligence is no match for dogged determination, but what it took to save wild lands was courage.**

ABORIGINAL SIPSEY

Mortor Rock in Sipsey Wilderness

American Indian people have lived in the area of Sipsey River for some 10,000 to 12,000 years; they left their stone tools, mortars, lap stones, flint projectile points, petroglyphs, trail remnants, and implements of occupation scattered across the forest. Evidence of aboriginal occupation can be found in numerous rock shelters, along the old trails, and in the sheltered valleys across the Sipsey Wilderness and William B. Bankhead Forest of the Black Warrior Mountains.

Indian people lived in harmony with the land for thousands of years before the coming of white settlers; most whites moved into area to claim the land, build their homes, and to make permanent settlements in the area after the Creek Indian War was over in March 1814 and after the Turkey Town Treaty of September 1816. White settlements and permanent European occupation in the area is less than 200 years old, but white folks seem to think they were the first here.

Many aboriginal Indian trails and paths crossed the Sipsey area during some ten thousands of years of occupation. These trails included the High Town Path that became portions of the Leola, Cheatham, Ridge, and Byler Roads; the Old Buffalo Trail which later was known as Doublehead's Trace and portions of the Byler Road; the Sipsie Trail that became portions of the Cheatham Road and later Highway 33; Black Warriors' Path that was used as a Creek Indian removal route through the forest along the Leola Road; and many other minor trails leading to the numerous springs and bluff shelters scattered across the Sipsey drainage.

Sipsie Trail at the east edge of Mclemore Cemetery in Bankhead Forest

During historic Indian occupation of the Sipsey area, the Lower Cherokee, Upper Creek, Chickasaw, Shawnee, and Yuchi formed a Chickamauga Confederacy which controlled the Black Warrior Mountains of North Alabama. Many of the members of the Chickamauga were of mixed Celtic and Indian ancestry; Indian traders came into Indian country and married into the tribes.

By 1800, all the North Alabama tribes were controlled by mixed-blood chiefs; John McDonald, the Scots Irish grandfather of Chief John Ross, was a British agent working under John Stuart, Southern Superintendent of British Indian Affairs. John McDonald and Alexander Cameron supplied all the tribes within the Chickamauga Confederacy with arms, gun powder, ammunition, and other materials to fight the American settlers encroaching on to their ancestral lands.

Chickamauga Cherokee Chief Doublehead lived at the head of Elk River Shoals at Doublehead's Town on the Tennessee River and controlled the Sipsey area from 1750 until his death on August 9, 1807. For thousands of years before Doublehead walked this land and ruled it with an iron fist, the Kinlock Rock Shelter was one of the sacred sites of the prehistoric Indian people of North Alabama; later historic Indians and Indian mixed-bloods revered Kinlock as sacred and holy.

In 1967, an archaeological test pit was dug by David Lloyd DeJarnette (6/2/1907-1/16/1991) from the University of Alabama and assisted by local historian and archaeologist Spencer Waters of Moulton, Alabama. The archaeologists made the test pit as far back in the cave of the Kinlock Rock Shelter as the group could go. The archeological team discovered paleo projectile points; Spencer Waters told me about the dig and gave me a copy of the letter from DeJarnette. Spencer said, "*We never got a full blown archaeological dig authorized for Kinlock Rock Shelter.*" DeJarnette, Waters, and other archaeologists considered Kinlock to be a premier petroglyph site in the southeast.

Kinlock, which lies just outside the Sipsey Wilderness Area, was on the summer route of the Old Buffalo Trail which passed by Kinlock Spring and the Kinlock Rock Shelter. After Doublehead upgraded the Old Buffalo Trail into a wagon road from the mouth of Bluewater Creek to Franklin, Tennessee, the route became known as Doublehead's Trace; historic markers today, refer to the route as Doublehead's Road or the

Nashville Trace. Byler's Old Turnpike ran along portions of Doublehead's Trace west of the present-day Sipsey Wilderness Area.

Kinlock Rock Shelter

Kinlock—The Sacred Fire

Terra Manasco was asked to write in her own words what Kinlock Rock Shelter meant to her and her family. The following by Terra shows how deeply she and the Jim and Ruth Manasco Family believe and feel about the Kinlock area adjacent to the Sipsey Wilderness. Kinlock Rock Shelter was so sacred and holy to the family that the ashes of their offspring were scattered in this significant Indian site:

My name is Terra Manasco and I am the eighth descendant of Man Drowned a Bear, who once walked this forest. Like others who still keep the old ways here in this area, the years have forced my skin pale through a genetic sieve but still the Sacred Fire rides my veins.

75

> **The years have forced my skin pale through a genetic sieve but still the Sacred Fire rides my veins. I was born with the sound of the Little Mysteries in my ears and I was raised in the forest, taught by my parents the ways of the plants and animals before I was to know the ways of my people.**

I was born with the sound of the Little Mysteries in my ears and I was raised in the forest, taught by my parents the ways of the plants and animals before I was to know the ways of my people. My family has Cherokee ancestry on both sides. My mother's people once lived in Brown's Valley here in the Bankhead while my father's people were forced west on the Trail of Tears. Both of my parents passed the Fire and the Way of the Four Twisters on to me.

I have known since birth that I would one day carry the spark for the old voices that still sing in this forest, for the drums that still float here in the wind. And so it came to pass one day, that I too became a "Keeper of That Which Must Be Kept" and like my father before me and others before him, I made the same vows that have come down through the centuries and across bloodlines.

I tell you this because today "looks" are sometimes deceiving to the outside world but from my own experience I can say that the old power is still here in this forest, carried in the veins of many of the people you see around you today. One place in the forest where the old power drums loudest is a place known to the public as Kinlock Antiquities. This place was and is a power spot used for sacred purposes, including what is known in modern terms as the 'vision quest' as well as the ceremonial acknowledgement of the solar cycles.

Terra Manasco

It was the Uchee, who called themselves the Children of the Sun, who first used this site to Walk the Rainbow. Inducing themselves into a trance of blue-blackness formed by a series of sacred number patterns, a cord of white light would shoot out from their navels and arc out into the universe. It was upon this cord that they Walked the Rainbow and visited many worlds. The symbols carved on Kinlock's rocks are the magic symbols used in the trance as well as recreations of spirits encountered beyond the Rainbow.

The Uche were the first to walk into this blind canyon and to feel the power that moved here in this crack between the material and spirit worlds, but many others would come behind them, including the Cherokee, who would regard this place as sacred.

I have long considered it my personal responsibility to see that this place is protected and "remade" in both song and ceremony, and I know of others who feel from the depths of their hearts this same sense of guardianship.

I have gone through many seasons and stood alone in this canyon innumerable times as the dawn broke here. I have re-

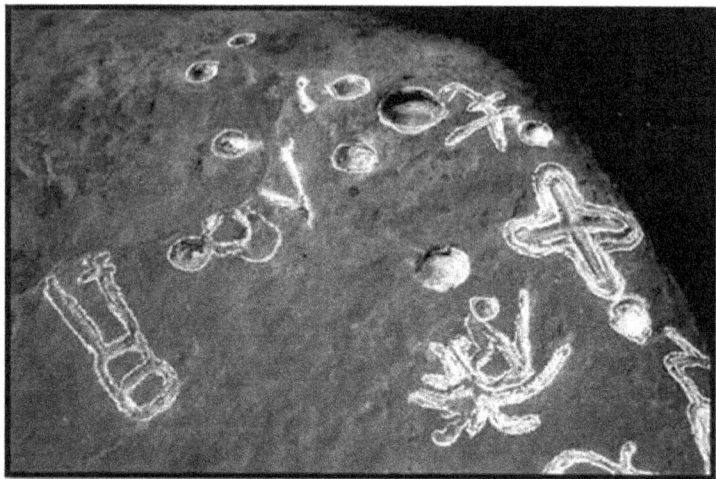

Kinlock Symbols

joiced at the times when its power was strongest and I have wept bitter tears to see it desecrated by pothunters and graffiti and now I must worry about proposed clearcuts nearby which if carried out by the Forest Service, for me would be akin to murder.

Today, I am one of many that come to this sacred place, both alone and in groups for the beauty and power that it offers. This place, by all that I hold holy, is a place that should exist in the world both for its own sake as well as for the lives of the people who still feel its Medicine.

In a world that increasingly has fewer and fewer solutions to the madness that spins out of rhythm around us, Kinlock has answers, and no Destroyer can take those answers from the world as long as one grain of its sandstone bluff remains in this forest.

I and others like me, have vowed to protect this place for we know that if we lose Kinlock, we will break the Turtle's heart, because the day the drums die in the wind in the Bankhead is the day an irreplaceable part of the Sacred Fire that burns yet in our veins will be lost forever.

Like Terra Manasco, many of the mixed-blood Indian descendants know that Kinlock is sacred and holy; we will not allow that sacred fire to be lost forever. Even though we too have had our skin whitened by the genetic sieve, our children and their descendants will get whiter until all melts away like tracks in the snow on a warm spring day. The great Chickamauga War Chief Dragging Canoe described it this way, "*Whole Indian nations have melted away like snowballs in the sun before the white man's advance.*"

It is my hope that our younger generations of mixed-blood children will always remember Kinlock and hold on to their Indian heritage and culture. As the Cherokee leader John Ridge wrote in 1835, "*Our blood, if not destroyed, will win its course in beings of fair complexion, who will read that their ancestors became civilized under the frowns of misfortune, and the causes of their enemies,*" so lives the remnants of the mixed-blood Indian people of Sipsey.

SIPSEY WILDERNESS AREA

In the Bankhead National Forest just north of Double Springs and south of Moulton, Alabama, there is a 25,986 acre tract of wilderness with another 5,000 acres of scenic river and canyon lands preserved by Congress to remain in its natural state. It is a place where no wheeled vehicle may travel, and where no tree may be cut. It is the Sipsey Wilderness Area.

The Sipsey Wilderness Area is of such scenic beauty and natural interest that it could not be described in a single article. Each of the many canyons has its own point of special interest. Jim Manasco said, *"Through visits to these canyons, one at a time, I hope that subsequent articles may awake in the readers a sense of value in the wilderness concept. It belongs to the people and it is here on our back doorstep of North Alabama."*

Sipsey Wilderness is found in the southwestern portion of Lawrence County and northwest Winston County. Many people enjoy the beauty of one of North Alabama's greatest natural

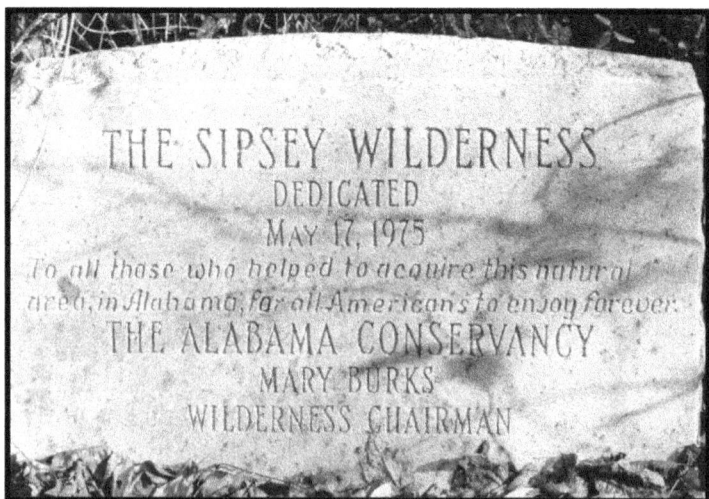

THE SIPSEY WILDERNESS
DEDICATED
MAY 17, 1975
To all those who helped to acquire this natural area in Alabama, for all Americans to enjoy forever.
THE ALABAMA CONSERVANCY
MARY BURKS
WILDERNESS CHAIRMAN

resources, the Sipsey Wilderness Area of William B. Bankhead National Forest that lies in the heart of the Black Warrior Mountains. Sipsey River Picnic Grounds are located on Sipsey River and the Cranal Road crossing; Cranal Road is the south border of the wilderness. Many people not only hike in the wilderness, but also drive along Highway 33 and the Cranal Road to enjoy the fall colors and splendors of the Sipsey Wilderness.

Believe it or not, there is a sign, a map and marked routes that will allow you to drive around the boundary of the Sipsey Wilderness in your car. But for some reason, the sign was placed so far off the road you cannot find it, placed on a road that no one uses to get to the wilderness. To find this secret sign, follow Highway 33 north from Double Springs. After entering Lawrence County, you will pass Cranal Road to the picnic grounds and go to the next road on your left. This is Northwest Road and is marked with a small green sign that reads "BLACK WARRIOR WILDLIFE EQUIPMENT SHED." Turn left, or west, on this road and you will find the sign about a quarter mile into the woods.

It would be wise to just drive these routes to familiarize yourself with the boundaries before you do any hiking in the wilderness. This is a very scenic drive and seeing the forest is well worth the trip. The road was built in the 1930s and is a gravel all-weather road with turn-outs. It would also be to your benefit to learn some of the landmarks in the wilderness proper by name. In the event you ever need help. The names of many sites in the wilderness are those recognized by the forest rangers and many in the general public.

When the first white settlers came to this forest in the early 1800s, some of it was already inhabited by mixed-bloods living in their aboriginal ancestors homelands. The old Indian names had just about vanished with the exception of Sipsey River. The word Sipsey is an Indian word that means poplar tree and is the only Indian name in the whole wilderness area. Sipsey River Canyon cuts the wilderness in half, east to west. You have to refer to the name of the stream coming into the Sipsey to be able to locate anything in the canyon.

Sightseeing, hiking, canoeing, bird watching, hunting, and horseback riding are only a few of the many outdoor recreational activities available to visitors from all over the Southeastern United States. The Sipsey Wilderness is the place for those who want to get away from modern conveniences without the sound of traffic, telephones, and TV's, but instead listening to the songs of warblers, the hammering beaks of woodpeckers, the hoot of the great horned owl, the howl of a lone coyote, and the sound of water running over rocks and boulders in the many streams flowing through this portion of the Black Warrior Mountains. Avid outdoorsmen cherish the stimulating sounds, sights, and smells that only Mother Nature can provide to those who visit the Sipsey Wilderness Area.

The United States Forest Service has designated and established trails for hiking, horseback riding, and horse or mule drawn wagons. These trails and roads provide access to secluded sandstone cliffs, wonderful waterfalls, fantastic fall foliage, beautiful wildflowers, and tremendous trees. Designated hiking trails begin at Borden Creek Bridge on the Bunyan Hill Road, Sipsey River Picnic Area on the Cranal Road, Gum Pond Road Trailhead, Braziel Creek Road Trailhead, Thompson Creek Bridge on the Northwest Road, Johnson Cemetery Road on the Cranal Road, and other numerous access sites.

A hiker can spend a few hours or a few days hiking the trail systems in Sipsey Wilderness. McDougal Hunter's Camp is a campground for those hunting or hiking in the area. Outside the wilderness, a system of horse trails begins at Owl Creek Horse Camp and contains many miles of connected riding loops, but none connect directly to the wilderness; although, the new addition to Sipsey Wilderness can be used by horse riders or mule drawn wagons. The wilderness access to wagons is along old existing roads and could provide rides for young, old, and disabled individuals through the most scenic portion of our Black Warrior Mountains.

In addition to various types of trails and roads in the Sipsey Wilderness Area, primitive wilderness camping is available to those who really want to get away without driving for hours. Two sites that are strongly recommended for wilderness camping is Bee Branch and Ship Rock; these areas are not totally isolated, but have great sandstone bluffs and shelters located on either side of the canyons.

Bee Branch and Big Tree

On the closed portion of the Bunyan Hill Road about three-quarters of a mile east of its intersection with Northwest Road, a pile of dirt blocks and marks the entrance to an old logging road. Here, where the road use to widen from use as a parking lot once was a sign that read "BEE BRANCH TRAIL." The sign is gone now but the trail is still there. It leads to the Big Tree.

This is a type of tree the Indians called "Sipsey" and of all its names that is probably the best. It is one of the most common trees in Alabama and is known locally as the yellow poplar, tulip poplar, or the tulip tree.

The tree is not a poplar, it is a wild magnolia. Its botanical name is *Liriodendeon tulipifera*. Liriodendron means lily

tree and tulipifera means to strike a tulip. This is in reference to the leaves having a striking resemblance to the shape of a tulip.

This is the rip-off tree of the American nurserymen. You read of the tulip tree in their catalogues and of the flowers likened to tulips. You see the big name and order one. What you receive is a plain old "yeller poplar." This tree is little more than a weed insofar as its numbers in Alabama.

The Big Tree first becomes visible as you reach the lip of the canyon. At first you do not realize how big the tree is because you are looking at it from the top down. Here on the rim the waterfall holds your attention as it drops 100 feet into the rock-strewn Bee Branch Canyon. It is not until you have snaked your way down the trail to the foot of the tree that you realize just how large it is.

This big bee tree is 21 feet in circumference four feet up its trunk and is almost that big around 150 feet further up. This hollow giant is estimated to be 550 to 600 years old. It makes man look small in many ways. Not only has it witnessed the history of America, but was here even before Columbus was born.

The limbs at the top have broken off from their own weight and there are now holes that open to the main cavity. Here the wild bees have lived unmolested by man for centuries, protected by the size of the tree. Bee Branch took its name long before any white man saw it.

Here in the cracks of the boulders at the Big Tree lives the Little Peter's Fern. It is a rare plant that was discovered in this forest and named for its discoverer, Judge Thomas Peters of Moulton.

A short walk down the canyon through the virgin cove of hardwood brings you to a stand of hemlocks. Hemlocks are not very strong and are blown over long before their time. No one knows how large one would grow if fully protected from storms. There is here a hint, however, for growing next to the face of a high vertical cliff is a giant. It is 12 feet in circumference at eye level. It is botanically unrecorded, but might be the largest of its kind.

Under the overhang near the hemlocks are fragments of old clay jugs and rusty wooden barrel rings. Some moonshiner in the years gone by must have had his still raided here. There are old still sites in countless hollows and are the things for which this country was once famous.

Also near this site was once an old tub mill that settlers on the west rim used to mill their corn. The only sign of the mill is a very faint sled track where the meal was dragged up the hill, and it can only be seen if you know where to look. Soon it will be gone. Nature kindly heals all wounds.

Bee Branch Canyon is Y shaped and the Big Tree part is the smallest. Where the branches come together there is no hint of the box canyon to the west. It is the longest section of the canyon. It is in this section of Bee Branch that most people get lost; Big Tree fork is the shortest arm of Bee Branch Canyon and is the east branch of the Bee Branch Trail that leads to the Big Tree. Bee Branch of the Sipsey Wilderness Area is located primarily in Section 26 of Township 8 South, Range 9 West. Bee Branch is a deep canyon located northeast of Sipsey River. The area is probably the most primeval site in the Black Warrior Mountains. Most of the canyon was protected by the United States Forest Service as early as 1919.

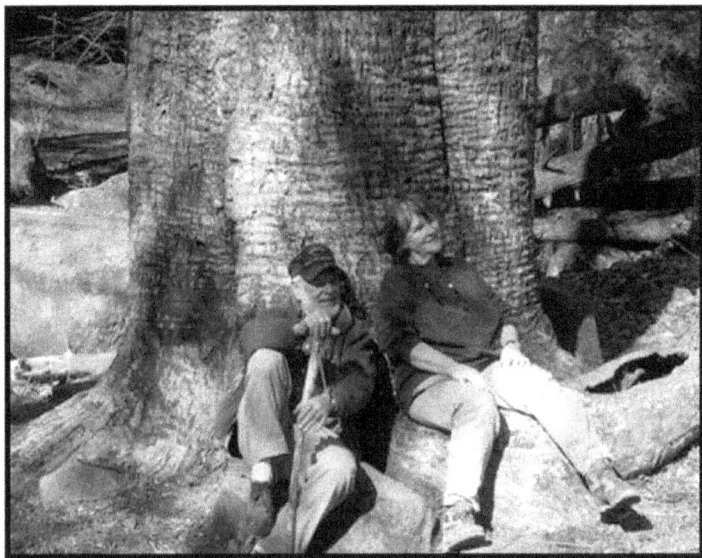

Jim and Ruth rest on roots of the Big Tree

Lost may not be the proper word. This canyon has few exits and is so long that it takes a while to get out. Those going into the canyon late are caught by dark before they can find their way out. They are trapped rather than lost.

It is no big deal. The next morning they come wandering out. Mothers don't understand though.

Bee Branch and Big Tree Route

Rex Free of Moulton, Alabama, describes the best and quickest route to the Big Tree; the following is courtesy of the blog Rex writes for the people that follow his writings.

Rex Free says, *"Of all the… requests I get… the majority seem to all ask the same question "What is the best route to get to the Big Tree? I decided it was time to help some folks out… I cannot answer all… but maybe I can answer most of them here…*

First, of ALL the reports of people getting lost in the Sipsey Wilderness, most all of them center on people either going or coming from the Big Tree. The majority of people knows and respects the woods, but even the most skilled woodsmen have been *turned around getting to this giant icon of the south. Being respectful of Mother Nature and her elements are the key to taking off on this trip. A pair of sneakers and a bag of M&M's will probably get you there and back, but if anything goes wrong, you might just find yourself spending the night on the ground, or hovering by a fire*

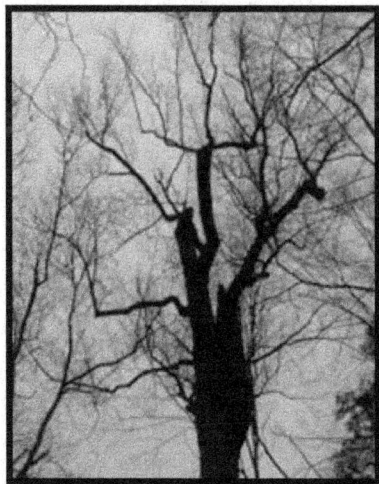

wishing you had told someone where you were going while search parties are planted throughout Bankhead looking for you.

If you decide to take a hike to the Big Tree whether to camp or to just take a day hike, PLAN AHEAD! Pick a FULL day to go do this. Don't hit the woods at 2:15 p.m. and expect to dash in and come out. Don't take small children that will tire out fast, otherwise, plan on sore shoulders and a very ill child by the end of the day. There is NO RELIABLE CELL PHONE coverage in the Sispey Wilderness Area.

If you are an amateur radio operator, there is a repeater in the forest you can reach. It is the 146.960 Moulton repeater. There is also the 442.425 repeater but does not cover the wilderness area as good. Both are sponsored by the Bankhead Amateur Radio Club. They are open for all amateur radio operators to use. KNOW the area or get familiar with the area to some extent. I am a member of some clubs that hike and kayak, and I am totally amazed that some people have NO idea of where they are, how to get out, or even where to start. They simply just "go with the crowd". Most of the time that is fine;

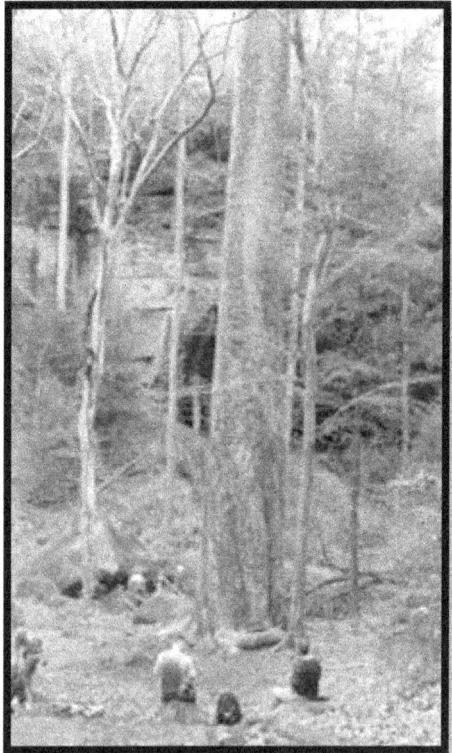

at one point in your life, it won't work, and YOU have to take care of yourself.

On this trip, take lots of water, some food, a coat, jacket, and/or rain jacket, and a good pair of boots, not tennis shoes. Be prepared to get sweaty, dirty, and use every muscle in your body. This is a moderate to extreme hike for most people, so if you only hike in the city parks or on flat ground, you are in for a surprise! The reward however if you go and make it (and you will), will give you the honorable title of working for a goal and saying 'I've been there!'

Nothing pleases me more than taking people to go see the Big Tree. Many groan, complain, and fuss the entire way at me and everyone else. Within one month after the trip, they are so glad they went, and will proclaim 'it was worth every mile.' I lost count at 14 times going there, so this place is old hat to me. Do I carry a GPS and map with me after this many times? YOU BETCHA, and I ALWAYS WILL!

There are about four ways to get to the Big Tree, but to cut down confusion; I am going to cover three of the most popular routes. The third is my preferred and the shortest. The MAIN route that most folks take is by sticking to the trail. They park at Cranal Road and Take Trail 201 or 202 and make their way down to 204 and camp along the way. Locals call this the 'city slicker route' with all due respect. This is the route that would seem the most 'logical' to follow given you don't know the area and you follow the U.S. Forest trail system. This is the killer hike route and most folks that do this, do it to camp. A few wandering soles take this route for a day hike; they come back calling it 'the day hike from Hades.'

Another route is to park at Thompson Creek Trailhead, and follow Forest Service Trail along Thompson Creek taking FS206 and hit 209, and it will take you to the Big Tree. This appears to be the most popular route. This carries you through the King Cove area and a popular landmark called Ship Rock. Many camp here because it is basically a huge rock that looks like the bow of a ship. There is also the Eye of the Needle in this area. It is a hole in the rocks near Ship Rock that allow you to cut through the cliff area and shorten your long route around Ship Rock down by Thompson Creek. On this popular route, you will meet your friends, neighbors, your brother, your cousin, your cousin's mother, etc. I am just kidding, but you get it now. This is the major highway route that many take to the Big Tree and camp along the way. Another blog is written about this route, so read it if you are interested in this 'major highway route' that most folks take. It is 5.5 miles one way and is relatively flat. If you like this route, then use it. If you want shortest time and least distance, then read on further!

For this blog, we will focus on my favorite route introduced to me back in 2002. It is off any 'official' U. S. Forest Service Trail map, and cuts time and distance in exactly half. It is a mere 2 miles in or a 1.5-2 hour walk in, and the once barely visible foot-path, is a 'pig trail' of high foot traffic that many are taking now. The first thing to do is get you a Sipsey Wilderness Map available at most any local store around the forest. Read this blog and then study the map. I have uploaded some pictures of my GPS tracks on here but they may not show up good enough for many. Look on your map and find Thompson Creek Trailhead. FS 206 and FS 208 start here. It is at the end of the Northwest Road. Park your vehicle here and tell your friends at home this is where you are parking.

Take FS Trail 206; follow on this trail with Thompson Creek on your right side. Soon you come to a stream crossing that feeds into *Thompson Creek. This stream is in White Oak Hollow; cross the stream, pick the trail back up for about 200 feet, and the trail continues on beside Thompson Creek and has a sign pointing to the right telling you that 206 is to the right. This is where you 'part your ways' with the FS trails. You will notice a Y in the road at this point; you will bear to your left and start going up White Oak Hollow.*

You are leaving the U.S. Forest Service Trail 206, but no worries; your hiker friends have beat this trail to a pulp so you can easily see the trail. Follow the trail going up into White Oak Hollow; it follows beside this tributary stream and to the right of it. Soon, you will see that the trail is starting to go up the hill and to the right side of White Oak Hollow. You will see that it starts going straight up and is heading to the southeast of White Oak Hollow. It is here on this incline, that your stamina will be tested! The incline gets steeper and steeper as you are proceeding up and out of White Oak Hollow to the southeast. You can stop along the way (and you will be out of breath), and notice the pretty rock out croppings to your right. A stream you start joining and winding back and forth across leads you; it directs you in the right direction as you are making your way out of White Oak Hollow. When you get to the top of the hill and look back down on White Oak, you will notice you are standing on an old logging road at the top of the canyon. It leads you to some awesome hideout camps, but sorry, not to be talked about in this blog! After you sit down and take a short break with water, you then head on southeast and cross the logging road. You are headed back down into another canyon. Follow closely the trail and stay on it; if you are not familiar with the area, it is from here on that people get their 'doubts,' but have no fear, a solid trail is in front of you if you pay attention.

Let's head on....The trail that goes down into the canyon used to be nice and straight. With hurricanes in the past pushing trees down, it has turned this part of the trip into a zigzag cross country course. As of this writing (August of 2011), it is still in this shape. It is kind of aggravating having to zigzag back and forth but will change with time as the downed trees start to rot away.

When you descend down, you will go from open forest land and slowly start getting into my most favorite part of the Bankhead National Forest, the hemlocks! The trail will start to take you down into a steep part of the canyon, and this is where it can get dangerous, depending on your skill and hiking level. This is the only area where I preach a sermon to those with me to take your time and be careful. The trail takes you down into a small waterfall and very slippery part. You have to negotiate down into the stream bed area and then follow the rocks of the stream bed for about 100 feet. Take your time here! People have left behind ropes to help you get down, and they may or may not be there. When you walk on the rocks, be very careful. I know a lady that went with us on one hike and slipped and fell on her bottom here. She felt pains from it for a year. After you have successfully negotiated this area, you are home free now as far as

difficulty levels. This area when you come back up will go much faster than coming down. It is harder to come down a slick slope and rocks than it is to climb up one.

After you reach the bottom of the canyon, take the time to walk slowly and admire the tall and beautiful bluff walls of the canyon to your left. The stream you came down will be on your right. This area is a good place to just stop and absorb some of the hemlocks and cliffs. As you walk on down the trail, you will come to a stream you will have to cross. It feeds into the stream to your right and they merge together here. This is WEST Bee Branch and this is the area where many folks get turned around and shortly after become lost. Cross this stream and DO NOT TURN LEFT. Many people do this. You will want to cross the stream and continue on downstream with the stream remaining on your right.

If you were to turn left and march up West Bee Branch, you are going the wrong way! They do it so much that there is a trail beat down going on the right side of West Bee Branch! Wrong way folks! Many people do this and get into really rough country with the dense foliage; they get turned around and get confused. Most simply give up and return back to the truck or car. Where they went wrong is turning left at the first stream (West Bee Branch) and they should be going on down further to turn left on East Bee Branch.

Continuing on our hike, as you walk the heavily beaten trail with Bee Branch on your right, you will come down to a flat area on the other side of the creek. Before you get to this flat area though, you will notice lots of trees down through this area as well. A 'microburst' from a storm sent many trees down beside the stream and across the trail. It too, zigzags back and forth. There is going to be a small little eight foot wide hole in the middle of the trail (about 4 foot deep) you will have to climb down in and back up along this trail. Again, take your time through this. As you come down to the flat area off to your right on the other side of Bee Branch, this is going to be the intersection of East Bee Branch and Bee Branch. The trail runs right into East Bee Branch and Bee Branch will be on your right.

After crossing East Bee Branch, you turn left NOW, and walk UP East Bee Branch. The trail is on the right side of East Bee Branch and makes its way up the canyon, slowly gaining elevation up above East Bee Branch. The trail is about a half of a mile long and leads you right to the Big Tree.

Looking back on where we have come from: The most important thing I can stress here is when you come down from the slick rocks and canyon with ropes I talked about, do not take the first stream you cross to the left; cross it and go on down to the second stream and THEN turn left heading up into the canyon. Do this and you will not get lost as so many do.

While you are at the Big Tree, but sure and check out the two massive waterfalls that are nearby that add 'icing to the cake' rewarding you for your long walk. Take the time to eat your lunch there, taking in the scenery and the sounds of the waterfalls. Notice the orange iron ore seeping out from the canyon walls, an element used in making steel by the old timers of long ago. Also notice a rather large 'ball like' hole in the side of the canyon beneath the largest waterfall. Strange?

If you are adventurous, work your way up the canyon to the top where you can look down at the Big Tree and the canyon. This is better to do in the wintertime where you can see further.

Plan your trip, take water, plan on leaving Thompson Creek Trailhead about 9-10 a.m. to start your journey, and plan on getting out about 4-5 p.m. This is for day hikers. If you are over-

East Bee Branch Falls

night backpacking, well, I could write 6 blogs on things to do and more places to go on that, so I will save that for another day. I hope you enjoy your trip should you decide to go.

If it helps you any, I have taken some elderly men in their 70's on this hike. They were in good shape and they all made it fine. Just prepare yourself for sore muscles the next day. This shorter route is far more strenuous than the relatively flat 5.5 mile route, but will take half the time!

I hope this blog has been helpful to you. If so, set a date on the calendar and get going! I prefer winter months to do this myself. There is far more to see with the leaves gone and no ticks, chiggers, snakes, and mosquitoes. Everyone has their own special times they want to go so any time will do. I hope you get to see this 'giant icon' that attracts everyone in the South. If you do, then you can say 'I have been there!' the next time someone mentions 'The Big Tree.'"

Rex Free was gracious enough to let us use his detailed description of the short cut to the Big Tree. If you follow his directions and suggestions, you will have a safe and enjoyable trip to the big yeller poplar, as people in this area have called it for years.

Bee Branch is a forked canyon with seasonal and beautiful waterfalls in each fork. The Bee Branch Falls plunge from 50 feet above the canyon floor. Both forks are virtually box canyons forming a small creek that flows into Sipsey River. The eastern fork of the canyon features the largest yellow poplar in the Southeastern United States. The whole canyon is a botanical garden of a virgin gorge in the Black Warrior Mountains.

> **It is a place where history is stacked in layers. It is a canyon with no name, a cave with no name, a waterfall with no name: A place called Saltpeter Furnace.**

The west branch of Bee Branch is most unusual, but it must wait for another day... and night. We are headed elsewhere, downstream to a still of a different kind, to a canyon so small that it attracts little attention. It is a place where history is stacked in layers. It is a canyon with no name, a cave with no name, a waterfall with no name: A place called Saltpeter Furnace.

Saltpeter Furnace

Saltpeter furnace is a horseshoe bluff located on the first branch on the north side of Sipsey River just upstream from Bee Branch. The area was used during the Civil War for the production of black powder.

Walking up the Sipsey River from the mouth of Bee Branch, a person can easily spot mink and raccoon tracks in the wet

> **Yet this place, where the mountain lion and wolf out-numbered the people...**

sand banks. Beaver slides tell of night-time activity here where the river forces its way around the boulders. Everything is peaceful here. This place has always been wild and now, by act of Congress, it will stay that way. But it has not always been peaceful, for we are in the heart of the "Free State of Winston."

Those who lived here refused to fight for the Confederacy and seceded from Alabama to defend the Constitution. This did not set well with the majority of Alabamians. Small areas of dissension were quite common in all Southern states. Yet this place, where the mountain lion and wolf outnumbered the people, received more attention from the Union than all others.

Why? This place was a wilderness, described by General James Harrison Wilson as of "*almost absolute destitution.*" There were only a few people living in these hills. They had nothing and wanted nothing but to be left alone. The only thing they could offer the Union was loyalty. And were too few for that to account for the attention they received.

Here on the river, we are just two miles from Hubbard's Mill at Kinlock Falls. The road to the mill was the only road to this area and the road did not justify its overuse by Union troops. A most bizarre piece of history occurred on this road. A group of Union troops coming to the mill for supplies of corn and meal were ambushed. Yet they knew that on the other side of the hill was the Tennessee Valley, full of corn and mills. But they came here to a mill in the

> **A mill that running red-hot could barely feed one man and a half starved mule.**

wilderness that had a few little fields and a mill that running red-hot could barely feed one man and a half-starved mule... Why?

Six of those troopers died in the ambush; these union troops were buried in the black Hubbard Cemetery just a half mile north of David Hubbard's Kinlock home. And six men could almost have carried the whole grist mill away. It makes no sense.

What was the magic these hill people held over the Union that, on request, would bring the troops rushing to their aid? Why did Confederates not enter this area, here in the Heart of Dixie? One cannot help but feel that a whole chapter is missing in the history of the Free State...

Well, after walking up the river to the first small branch, one comes to a small canyon. It is known to a few local people as Saltpeter Furnace. Saltpeter Furnace is not recorded in written history, but it is here.

And here, in the Heart of Dixie, surrounded on all sides by Rebel forces, a band of Americans true to a cause were making black powder... for the Union.

Now, after 120 years, this place can be revealed for what it was. It was the smaller of two nitrate production areas in the Sipsey Wilderness. Had a tongue ever have slipped, the people in these hills would have been as-

David Hubbard House at Kinlock in 1930's

> **Had a tongue ever have slipped, the people in these hills would have been assaulted to a degree that would make Wounded Knee look like a Sunday school picnic.**

saulted to a degree that would make Wounded Knee look like a Sunday school picnic.

In this canyon, behind the waterfall, there is a cave which at times is still a home for bats. The entrance to the cave is at the bottom of a deep crevice. The trail markers in this case are the small rocks that had to be removed to reach the bat guano which would spill over the hillside by the falls. There are other excavation marks left from the old days.

Potassium nitrate, commonly called saltpeter, is a chemical product of decaying plants and animals. It is dissolved in water and the water is then boiled down; it accounts for 73 percent of the ingredients in gunpowder.

When saltpeter comes in contact with water and dissolves, it can only be detected by a salty taste, but it stains sandstone black. The rocks under the cliff here are black for the same reason the sand is black at saltpeter wells.

The old furnace is no more than 100 feet from the fall next to the face of the bluff. Saltpeter Furnace deserves a place in American history.

It is time to move on… to a 1936 Ford birdhouse at a place called Turkey Foot. The old car body has listened longer to the racket of baby birds than it did to the riotous humor of mountain people.

Turkey Foot Canyon

Turkey Foot Creek gets its name from the shape of its three branches; just about one half mile west from the Sipsey River Bridge on the Cranal Road, the creek has three forks on the south side of the Cranal Road that branch off in the shape like a turkey's foot. On the north downstream side of Turkey Foot Creek is Mize Mill and waterfall; the waterfall is just a few yards from the road.

The bridge at Sipsey River Recreation Area is in the southeast corner of wilderness. From here, going west, the south boundary of the wilderness is 66 feet from the center of the blacktop on the right-hand side of the road. This section of Cranal Road was built in 1960. Prior to that, the road was a single-track gravel road that crossed this section of the forest following the route of the least resistance. It is here in this corner of the wilderness that Turkey Foot Creek enters the Sipsey River.

Wilderness areas are required to have at least 5,000 acres, which makes large portions of them hard to reach. A place like Saltpeter Furnace requires a six mile hike. So some people think they cannot see wilderness without more trouble than it is worth. Turkey Foot Creek will change their minds.

Once you have arrived at the parking lot, you are already there. A person standing on the bridge between the parking lots can see the creek coming in from the west, right under the bridge. It does not look like much here, and neither does the cut over the hollow it comes out of. Most folks walk by it quickly as possible to get to prettier places up the river. You never see anyone in this canyon, yet it is the most scenic little canyon in the entire wilderness.

Turkey Foot Creek Milling Stone

Start walking up the creek from the bridge and notice that it appears to get bigger as you go up it. A lot of the water is absorbed by the sand on the river bank and makes it look that way.

The bridge is out of sight after a few minutes and the walls of the cliffs start to close in. The brush suddenly changes to virgin hemlocks. It stirs you inside and you don't know just what caused it.

By following the bluff along the south side of the creek, you soon find yourself in an old Indian shelter. There, standing by the milling stone, you look down into the hollow along the creek that has changed little since the Indians sat here making their acorn meal bread and hickory nut butter.

You say to yourself, "What a surprise!" and walk out the other end of the shelter, directly into the rear end of a 1936 Ford sedan.

The old road came around this side of the mountain before the new road was built. The old gravel road circled to the old bridge, following the very lip of the canyon.

More than two decades ago, the old Ford came roaring down the road, became airborne in the loose gravel, and sailed over the cliff. The steep bluffs that kept timber men from cutting the trees also kept the owner from removing the car.

The driver later told me he was unable to get the car out and

was compelled to dismantle it and snake the parts out with a mule, leaving the body. The car had come down on its wheels, receiving little damage and looking as though it had just been put there. The body became home for the forest birds until one night when the sky turned green. The tornado dropped a tree across it. That night will be long remembered in Guin, Jasper, and Huntsville.

A little further up the bluff, across the canyon, a nameless creek falls into the canyon. This waterfall is possibly the most photogenic in the entire wilderness. This whole canyon is a photographer's dream.

By now you might wonder just what else this little canyon could offer. Walking a little further up you see Turkey Foot Falls. Here at the head of the canyon, the cars can still be heard on the highway above the falls. Here, under the bluffs, once creaked the waterwheel of Mize Mill.

Above the falls, the creek cut a deep trough in the sandstone, and man cut sockets into the sandstone to hold a hewn-

Mize Mill flow sets for logs

log dam that stabilized the water flow to the mill. After climbing to the top of the falls, you find you are on the highway. The canyon is only a half-mile long. It is best seen by taking a walk up one side and back down the other. You are never more than a few blocks from the parking lot.

A person can reach this canyon by taking Alabama 195 from Jasper to Double Springs. Go straight across U.S. 278 to Highway 33 without turning. After this section of road joins old Highway 33, take the next road to the left. If that is too confusing, from Double Springs point your car towards Moulton and make no turns till you come to the first paved road to left after entering Lawrence County; then turn left on the Cranal Road toward Sipsey River.

Parker Branch

Parker Branch is the hardest to get to and the prettiest to look at, from the upper falls to the lower falls and on down to the river; near the falls is an Indian rock shelter that contains a large mortar rock. The stream running through the canyon goes into Hubbard Creek; the creek is named in honor of David Hubbard who lived at Kinlock and was Federal

Commissioner of Indian Affairs for the Confederate States of America.

There is no easy way to get there. Parker Branch Canyon is the most isolated canyon in the wilderness. The ridge tops are at the 900-foot level and the branch at 600.

In most places, this 300-foot drop is almost straight down as it descends over three bluff lines. Getting down in the canyon is hard, coming out is worse. When you start out you are looking right into the hillside at such a grade you are in more danger of dragging your nose on the ground than you are falling down.

There are two ways of getting into the canyon, one is long and hard, the other short and difficult. Why then did we go there? We have been there before and there is no prettier place in the forest.

After some 30 years of wandering the forest, you learn how to get where you are going by bushwhacking. That is what they call it when you just take off as the crow flies, bee-lining it, hanging yourself on saw briars, falling over logs, getting

MORTAR IN PARKER SHELTER

slapped in the face with tree limbs, and crossing the creeks where you find them.

Knowing what lay ahead, we headed down Johnson Cemetery Road and then veered on an old log road the Forest Service calls 201. Everything in the forest seems to have a number on it. After walking 201 for a mile or so, we turned west into a solid wall of vegetation. Bushwhacking the ridge, we then dropped into a draw on top of the ridge, following this water course down the mountain. I had never been in this draw before but that made no difference as it could only go to the branch. No one ever goes in the off-trail places; they stay near the trails or streams.

It must have been like that in the past also for halfway down the hollow we found a whiskey still that not even the revenuers discovered. The old vat was made of sheet metal nailed to a wooden frame. The frame was on the inside so the heat did not affect it. With time the wooden frame rotted and it gently sank into the furnace.

After passing the still, we came to the first bluff line and worked our way down around the waterfall. Now dropping at a fast rate, we came to the second bluff line which had two waterfalls at the run over. This one was somewhat harder to get down than the first and we had to go back up the hill to find a way around it. Dropping further down the hill we came to the last bluff that drops to the branch and we could not get down. This happens regularly when bushwhacking. The top of the bluff was a tangled mass of mountain laurel. When this happens you start walking the bluff line looking for animal trails which always leads to a way down.

However, this trail led to a large dead tree that had fallen against the bluff and it was too risky to try. Crawling through the laurel backwards you learn quickly why the people of the mountains call these places laurel hells. The next animal trail led us down a series of door stepped waterfalls into the bottom of the canyon.

Crawling through the laurel backwards you learn quickly why the people of the mountains call these places laurel hells.

It had been my intention to bee-line a mile of underbrush with ridges that go in several directions, and come in at the cascades. I missed the cascades by less than a hundred feet. Next time I try it, I will likely come out in Cleveland, Ohio.

It is a hard trip down but once you are there you know that is was worth it. You just have to be careful for help is a long way off and slow coming, a twisted ankle and you stay there for a while.

This section of Parker Branch began with the cascades that could almost be called a falls. It then goes down through a solid rock canyon that has walls rounded by the branch. It is shaped like the bottom half of a pipe except it is huge. The hemlocks grow in places along the bluff where dirt has been carried downstream and deposited. Being mostly rock, though, the greenery is mostly ferns and mosses.

At the end of the span in the canyon, the whole branch is forced through a 12-inch gap between large boulders. The action of the water has created a large placid pool below the rocks. It is the kind of place you see only in the movies, wild, beautiful and untouched. But as pleasant as it was, we had to leave.

Starting up the branch there was a rustling in the leaves behind me. Jim said, "*I turned to see my wife with one leg miss-*

ing." An underground stream had washed a cave out and only the tree roots had held enough dirt to cover it. The unquestionable solid ground had given away and left one leg hanging in the cavern below.

My first thought was that she had ruined the pictures, then that she had broken her leg and would have to be carried out. It was then that I remembered I did not have a gun.

Next, I will come out of the canyon beneath the blooms of the laurel and cowcumber tree listening to the constant mully-grubbing I have to listen to from those people who just thought they wanted to go with me. At times, I am not so sure what I am doing there either.

Free from slippery rocks and crystal clear water, Parker Branch flows over solid rock; the only way to see the canyon is to wade the creek. The shrubs on the banks are too thick to walk through and at times there are no banks present. Many places the bluff walls drop into the stream bed on both sides leaving the stream as the only passage. There is no way you can walk Parker Branch without getting your feet wet so it is best just to get in the stream and walk it up the canyon. It is the best place to walk and offers the best views.

> **This I call "the place of the spinning rocks."**

One stretch of the creek bed near the cascades is flat and smooth as a sidewalk. This I call "the place of the spinning rocks." Here sand and water act together to drill pot holes in the bed rock. When a rock is dislodged from the bank and washed out on the flat bed rock, sand carried by the water begins to circle it. This action cuts round holes in the bed rock. With time the rock that started the process is eaten away leaving only the hole. These kinds of holes are often thought to have been made by Indians.

If you go to this area and see the rocks in these pot holes please do not remove them so others can see the same. You will find these holes in this area in all stages of progress but once rock is removed from the hole the action is stopped.

People have been coming to Parker for a long time. On a beech tree near the Indian shelter, someone carved his name and the date of February 13, 1881, over a hundred years ago. This carving is unusual in that it was not printed. There is another tree on the branch carved by Bill Tidwell in 1912. This is the year that the Bankhead National Forest was dedicated as the Cherokee National Forest and the name later changed.

The old land records show that this section of land that the branch flows through was never entered. I can only assume that the early visitors came to the canyon for the same reason that people do today as it is once again wilderness; just for the peace and quiet or maybe to hunt. Some recent visitors came a week ago for other reasons.

The Indian shelter that had two fire pits neatly rocked and a milling stone had remained just as the Indians had left it. Many people had seen the place and left it untouched. But last week the silence was broken by the sound of the pot hunters shovels. It is a shame that after all those years of the site remaining unspoiled, now that the area was finally preserved under law someone would ruin it.

There are a lot of people that dream of getting rich and somehow get it into their heads that the best way is to find a treasure. This leads them to think that the Indians had some. I define that kind of thinking as crazy. The Indians of Alabama had nothing that the average American today would consider of any value other than their land they stole all of those years ago.

There is a treasure here but few will find it. I know it is there for I have seen it in Parker Falls, in the blooms of the cowcumbers and mountain laurel. I have heard it in the rippling of the water and the distant muffled cry of a wood hen deep in a remote hollow. I have smelled it in the wind coming up from the creek where the swamp honeysuckles live, in the wiry root of the Virginia snake root and the wild ginger. People just do not realize how precious this little piece of real estate called the Sipsey Wilderness is. Twelve years ago a search was made to find a wilderness site in Alabama and this little place that is no bigger than a fly speck on a map was all that was left. You don't get a second chance with wilderness. It is either there or is not.

There is a treasure here but few will find it. I know it is there for I have seen it in Parker Falls, in the blooms of the cowcumbers and mountain laurel. I have heard it in the rippling of the water and the distant muffled cry of a wood hen deep in a remote hollow. I have smelled it in the wind coming up from the creek where the swamp honeysuckles live, in the wiry root of the Virginia snake root and the wild ginger.

I do get upset when people mistreat the wilderness but these are very, very few. The mass majority of people that go into the area are the best. They are really great about not littering or destroying any of it and treat it with loving care. Only rarely do we get a nerd carving his name for the world to see, and leaving his camping gear and garbage behind.

The best way to see Parker Branch is to come in from the south on the Johnson Cemetery Road and follow trail 201 to Sipsey River. Where this trail reaches the canyon bottom at the river you are in King Cove. This is the most unusual plant community in the wilderness and has a bluff shelter to spend the night in so no tent is needed. In the morning if you walk up the river to the first branch you are at the mouth of Parker. Parker Branch should have been named a creek rather than a branch because it is larger than many of the other streams in the forest that are called creeks.

Walking up the branch you will come to the cascades where the water runs over a rounded waterfall. Further up you will come to Parker Falls. Above this falls, the branch will fork. You should follow the left hand fork. This will lead you up hill to the black top road. Turn left on the black top and walk a hundred yards or so and you are back to your car.

Borden Creek

Borden Creek was named for the Christopher Borden family that lived in the area and was formerly known as the East Fork of Sipsey River; it is thought that Christopher Borden is buried in the Dement Cemetery in Borden Cove now known as Blankenship Cove. The old home of David Borden is in the center of the cove and has one of the largest limestone springs in the Bankhead Forest; the spring has a tremendous flow of fresh cold water throughout the year. David, 1/2 Cherokee, was the son of Christopher Borden.

Borden Creek Trail begins at the Sipsey River picnic area and follows upstream to where the river forks. It then follows the east fork till it reaches Bunyan Hill Road. The trail is 2.5 miles long and has one place that is hard to cross.

Here, where a waterfall drops twice into the river, the trail goes through a tunnel.

About a half mile from the Bunyan Hill end of the trail, a bluff blocks the route. Here, where a waterfall drops twice into the river, the trail goes through a tunnel. From the south the trail enters a hole in the face of the bluff and 40 feet later comes out under the water fall.

At one place the tunnel is a tight squeeze for an average-size man. The tunnel can be bypassed by going over the top, but that is as hard as going through it. This area of the canyon has been a favorite of botanists for many years. It was on this trail that Dr. Charles Mohr (December 28, 1824–July 17, 1901) found the lost yellow magnolia in 1882. He was given an honorary doctoral degree by the University of Alabama in 1893 in recognition of his work. This tree is exceedingly rare and was first found on the Savannah River in Georgia in the late 1700s. From this site in Georgia, some trees were taken to Europe for gardens.

Later the tree was reintroduced to the northern states from Europe. It was thought the tree was not seen in the wild again until 1913, but Dr. Mohr's records disprove that. His records show that he found it on the East Fork of the Sipsey River on the north boundary of Winston County in 1882.

Very few creeks in the wilderness were named and over the years were called by the names of the early settlers who lived near them. Borden's Creek and the East Fork are one and the same; Borden Creek got its name from Christopher Borden who settled in its upper valley coves in the early 1800s.

The yellow magnolia, *Magnolia cordata*, is fairly common in the wilderness but nowhere else; Andre Michaux, author of first flora of North America, found the *Magnolia cordata* in 1788, but some botanists say it is a subspecies of *Magnolia acuminata* while others say it is actually *Magnolia fraseri*. We hill folks in North Alabama still believe the rare magnolia of Sipsey Wilderness is truly the yellow magnolia or *Magnolia cordata.*

The easiest yellow magnolia tree to locate is growing on the southwest corner of the curved bridge on Bunyan Hill Road. It is the tree nearest the bridge and the creek. By standing on the bridge you can get a close look at the tree when it blooms. The tree blooms just as the first leaves start to appear. Other trees in the area bloom before any leaves appear. These rare trees are now assured a place to survive here in the wilderness, but one little bird that has in the past flitted through them may not.

Bachman's warbler has an olive green back and a yellow belly with

Bachman's Warbler

males having a black throat patch and crown of head; the bird may be extinct already, though it was seen in this forest as late as 1970. Nothing is known about this bird and the reason for its disappearance is unknown. Even if it is found, no one would know where it is going, for its nesting grounds are unrecorded at the present.

This trail is on the spring migration route of the warblers as they return from the South. These little birds are adapted to hardwood forests. As the hardwoods are replaced with pines, the birds are forced into smaller and smaller areas along the creeks. Their return through this forest is timed with the outbreak of insects which give them the strength to keep going.

At times a single tree will be alive with them. Usually it will be a beech tree on which the leaves have just come out. The flocks will have all different kinds mixed together as they compete for the worms.

The trail is also outstanding for its wildflowers. Along the creek banks grow the yellow trout lily, toothworts, shooting stars, and hepatica.

Here also, on a ledge near the tunnel, is the largest patch of shining moss in the wilderness. This moss is rare in our area but is still found regularly in the wilderness, though small patches, and never like it is in this area.

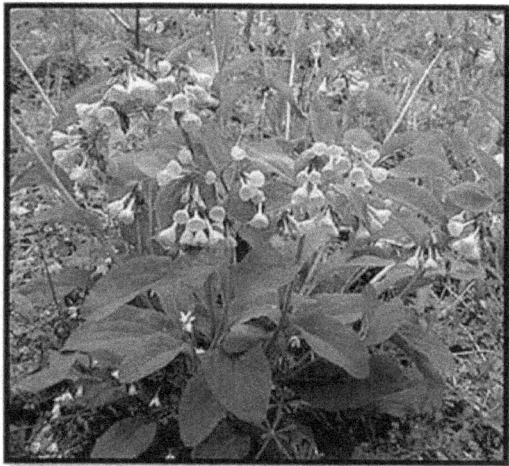
Virginia Bluebells

This trail is great in the spring for bird-watchers and botanists. I have hunted the wild turkey on this creek for years. In the spring, when the early greens come up along the river banks, the turkeys will come down off the ridge to feed on them.

After sitting and looking at the early greens for nearly 20 years, I finally had a little old lady come by and tell me they are Virginia bluebells. It was Blanche Dean, and it was she that introduced me to my forest. Prior to that day, I just thought I knew the forest. All I really knew was how to get from one place to another without knowing anything in between.

OTHER FOREST SITES

Blankenship Cove

The lower portion of Blankenship Cove is still an active farming site and is located primarily in Section 2 of Township 8 South and Range 8 West on the upper portion of Borden Creek. The cove was originally called Borden Cove, and settled by the family of Christopher Borden. The upper portion of Blankenship Cove extends through the northeast part of Sections 34 and 35 of Township 7 South and Range 8 West. David Borden, ½ Cherokee and son of Christopher, settled along portions of the lower cove adjacent to Borden Creek.

The cove is presently owned by Glenn Whisenant Family, who bought the property from the heirs of his Granddaddy Willis Blankenship; Willis's mother was Sarah Hannah Borden, ¾ Cherokee Indian, and granddaughter of Christopher. Two areas of the Blankenship Cove were known as the upper place and the lower place; Willis Blankenship lived on the lower place.

Ownership of land in the early days of settlement gave priority in naming some of the Coves of Bankhead. Many of the coves still found in Bankhead are beautiful isolated islands of open land nestled in the heart of the Black Warrior Mountains.

Buck Rough

Buck Rough is a term applied to a section of rough back country inhabited by deer and is hard to get in and out of. In Buck Rough, you can see five waterfalls from one spot. This beautiful canyon is the next hollow east of Bee Branch. The two canyons between Buck Rough and Falls Creek have no names.

Bunyan Hill

Bunyan Hill Branch drains from a mountain of the same name; a small early settler burial site is also known as Bunyan Hill Cemetery which is in the Sipsey Wilderness. The Bunyan Hill Road starts about one mile west of Highway 33; it turns off the Cranal Road and runs about three miles through the Sipsey Wilderness Area to the curved concrete bridge crossing Borden Creek. The Bunyan Hill Road is closed at the bridge at the Borden Creek Trailhead.

Falls Creek

Falls Creek is just what the name implies; the creek begins between the forks of the old Cullman Motorway and the old closed portion of the Bunyan Hill Road. A very short distance down the ravine from the junction of the two old roads that are now in the Sipsey Wilderness Area, the creek starts with a waterfall; just prior to reaching its terminal point on Sipsey River, it ends with a waterfall.

Indian Tomb Hollow

Indian Tomb Hollow is located primarily in Section 2 Township 8 South, Range 7 West on the northern edge of William B. Bankhead National Forest. In the distant hollows of Indian Tomb, the wood hen can be heard as the evening sun sinks behind the bluffs. Three gracious waterfalls of the southwest fork echo eternal sounds that formed the sandstone canyon containing vertical walls reaching to the sky. Looking down the canyon toward the northeast sandstone bluffs on either side of the canyon causes one to be in awe of the area because of its beauty.

Butch Walker at Indian Marker Tree

Early settlers and Indian mixed-bloods settled to the north and west of the hollow's southwestern fork. Several folks lived for a while in the old High House located on a small knoll at the mouth of Indian Tomb. Families of the Black Warrior Mountains would enter the hollow from the Alexander Motorway, Chestnut Ridge, Beulah, and High House Hill not only to view and enjoy the beauty of the area, but to dig roots, herbs, and hunt. It was in this same tradition that I, Rickey Butch Walker, was first introduced by my granddad Arthur Wilburn to the mysterious but beautiful Indian Tomb Hollow and the Indian Marker Tree. The Indian Marker Tree in Indian Tomb Hollow is a symbol considered sacred by the descendants of those aboriginal ancestors who once roamed the beautiful valley long before the coming of Europeans.

Mr. G. H. Melson tells of experiences he had as a small boy in Indian Tomb Hollow and is a wealth of information concerning an Indian fight occurring near the mouth of the famous canyon. He tells of his father working on the old plantation and passing down stories through many generations about the Indians of the area, the black slave cemetery, and the early mixed-blood Celtic Indian settlers who called the area home.

Over many years, the Gillespie family has traditionally been drawn to Indian Tomb. Not only does the family consider the area a sacred Indian burial site, but their ancestor, James Richard Gillespie, a veteran of the Creek Indian War, is buried in the Gillespie Cemetery. In addition, Gillespie Spring and Gillespie Creek, which runs through Indian Tomb Hollow, are named after the Gillespie Family of Lawrence County.

The ancient beech trees of Indian Tomb are a record of family traditions which have spanned over 200 years of time. From early Indian drawings and settler names, the beech trees of Indian Tomb bear record of visitation. The markings also indicate that much of the time spent in Indian Tomb was recorded in the numerous beech carvings located throughout the canyon.

A story called the "Battle of Indian Tomb Hollow" or "It-taloknak" was originally printed in *The Moulton Democrat* on November 7, 14, and 21, 1856. The articles, all of which occurred on a combination of the sacred seven, compose a beautiful love story that describes a fierce fight in Indian Tomb Hollow between the Creek and Chickasaw inhabitants of the Black Warrior Mountains.

Johnson Cemetery

Johnson Cemetery is in the Sipsey Wilderness Area about two miles northeast of the Cranal Road; the cemetery is still in use and is on a gated road off the Cranal Road between Wolf Pen

Cemetery and Parker Branch. The roads were formerly called motorways by the forest service.

King Cove

King Cove is a little obscure. Some say it is all of the Thompson Creek Canyon south of the bridge at the trail head on the Northwest Road. Jim Manasco says, "*I think it is a small cove on the south side of the Sipsey River across from the mouth of Thompson Creek; others say King Cove is much larger.*"

Rickey Butch Walker says, "*King Cove is located in Township 8 South, Range 9 West in Sections 22 and 27 of the southwestern portion of Lawrence County. King Cove lies adjacent to the forks of Hubbard and Thompson Creeks which is the beginning of Sipsey River in the western portion of Bankhead Forest. The King Cove extends up Thompson Creek to the forks of Tedford Creek and Mattox (Boyles) Creeks.*"

Ship Rock is found at the southeastern end of King Cove and is just east of the forks of Hubbard and Thompson. King Cove shows evidence of early Indian habitation. The Mortar Rock, located to the north across the creek from Ship Rock, contains five mortar holes and a huge nutting stone used by early Indian people. Local folklore tells of numerous arrowheads and spear points that could be picked up in the old creek bottom corn fields; the area is now in a stand of mature yellow poplar and other lowland tree species.

Bear Bottoms is the area between Hook Rock House and Ship Rock; the bottoms were some of the best corn ground in the forest. In the early settlement days, the area was so named because black bears would raid the ripening corn crops in the spring and summer; Hook Rock House was under a huge bluff that can be seen from eastern rock glade on the top of Ship

Rock when looking north up the Thompson Creek Valley. The rock shelter was the home of Jessie D. (Hook) Riddle; Jessie was a mixed-blood Cherokee Indian.

Huge nutting stone in King Cove

Kinlock Falls

Kinlock Falls is just off the Kinlock Road and is on Hubbard Creek; Kinlock was the name of the old David Hubbard plantation house that stood on the mountain above the falls.

Kinlock Falls is easily found by driving west on Cranal Road. When Cranal dead ends into Kinlock Road, turn right and go to the bridge. You would never know that the falls was there since it cannot be seen from the road, even though it is only 50 feet off the road.

The road is wide enough to provide ample parking just before you cross the bridge. A trail leads down the creek for about 50 yards to an overlook below the falls.

The oddity here is the fish. From the base of the falls to the Bankhead Lake lives a little fish known as the Warrior Darter. From the top of the falls upstream lives another darter and both of these are new to science. Neither has yet received a Latin name.

When these two species were introduced to the compilers of Alabama's endangered species list, one said "*describing species this rare is like writing their obituary.*"

> **Describing species this rare is like writing their obituary.**

One authority is convinced that the current attitudes of Federal Endangered Species Agencies will cause the fish above the falls to vanish before it is described. It requires clean water free of silt to survive and building log roads and cutting the timber will not help it any.

About halfway between the bridge and the falls you will see the old Hubbard's Mill; an early grist mill was located on the big flat rock above the falls. Here at the falls, you are with a few miles of the head of the Sipsey River drainage; this is the start of the Sipsey River Canyon.

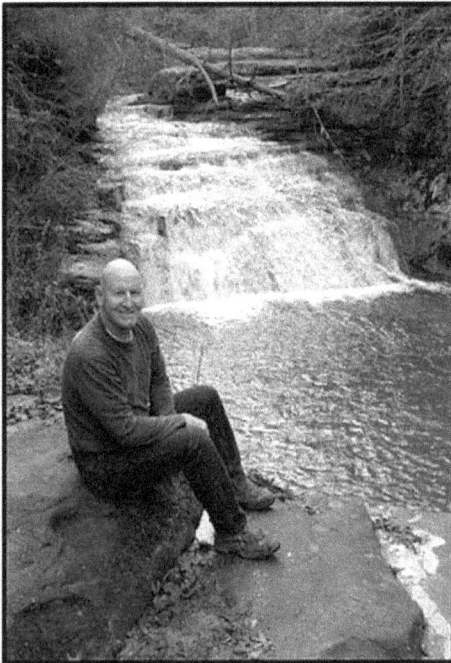

Butch Walker at Kinlock Falls

The evergreen trees that overhang the falls are Canadian Hemlocks. It is said that these trees seeded the northern forest. The theory is that the ice age killed all of the northern forest and only the trees in the Deep South survived. These trees then seeded the forest back through the original range.

This wilderness is truly a land of falling water. No one knows how many falls are in it. If you walk downstream from Kinlock you can see two.

The smaller falls comes through a rock chute before it drops into the river bed. Standing in front of the smaller one, Kinlock Falls is still in view.

Those of you who are interested in Kinlock Rock Shelter will find ancient rock carvings. This site is just outside the wilderness boundary at Kinlock Falls. It was a winter sunrise ceremonial site of prehistoric man; a people who were on the verge of developing a written language.

All nature is tuned in fine harmony. You can predict one thing by watching another. Watching the blooms of the dog-

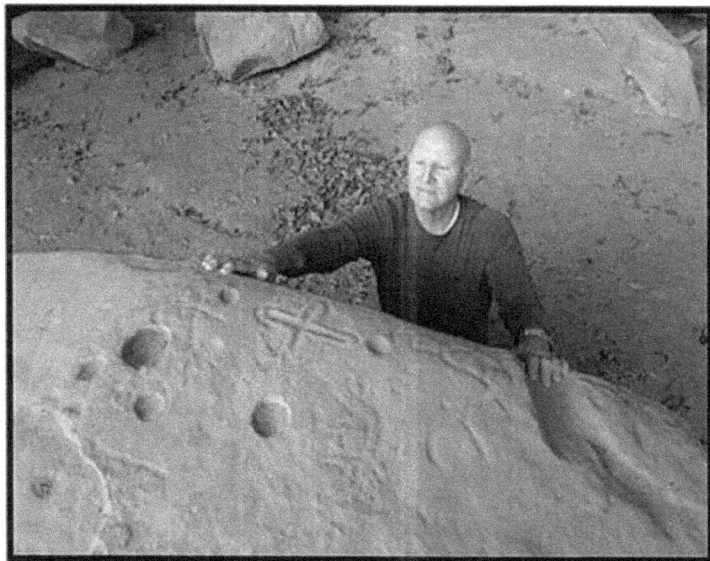

Butch Walker at Kinlock Petroglyphs

woods you know when the suckers will start their upstream run to spawn. Watching the suckers run you know when the folks will come to fish. Smiling faces, fish, and standing on a rock in the middle of nowhere, that is what wilderness is all about.

While the head of Sipsey Canyon is scenic, it is also primitive. The vista will quiet an appetite for natural beauty. But from the little falls on downstream, it is a different story. Take heed: there are no trails in this canyon and it is no place for the tenderfoot. The bluffs are high and the ledges are slick and narrow. It is dangerous – one slip and you've had it. To bypass the bluffs you have to bushwhack through laurel thickets and that is hard traveling.

If you have spent any time in the wilderness you may have noticed that the old timers shunned this part of the area, and with good reason. The rocky crags and thickets are the home of numerous canebrake rattlesnakes (velvet tails), some of record size. This area of the wilderness is the roughest and is marked on the map in part 5 with the number 8, Quillian Creek.

I can only recommend that you enjoy the wilderness where it has trails. Rattlesnakes are gentle when compared to other snakes and pose no threat to speak of on a trail. The danger of being bitten comes from stepping on one.

To bushwhack this type of terrain you have to watch every step and never drop your guard.

McDowell Cove

McDowell Cove of Bankhead Forest is located primarily in Section 4 Township 8 South and Range 8 West. McDowell Cove is on the upper drainages of Flanagin Creek and is one of the most beautiful canyons in the Black Warrior Mountains of Lawrence County. The Cove lies between Mountain Springs Road on the eastern ridge, Gum Pond Road located on the western ridge, and the Ridge road on the northern ridge. In the center of McDowell Cove, an Indian mound is found in the front yard of Jack McDowell's old log house. The flat level top of the mound actually lies immediately east of the dog trot style log cabin. The sides of the mound only rise some four to five feet at the highest point. Around the mound, numerous flakes of flint can be found. Throughout McDowell Cove, flint provides evidence of long term occupation of the cove by Indian inhabitants.

The area has been known as Wallis Cove, Wilkerson Cove, and after many of the other families that inhabited the area in the past; however, since Jack McDowell was the first Forest Ranger of Bankhead and one of the last to make the Cove his home, the area is widely accepted as being McDowell Cove. Wallis Cemetery, named after some of the Cove's first residents, contains the graves of four Civil War soldiers. Two old houses still stand in the flat valley—Jack McDowell's home and the Sanko Wilkerson home. The old Sally Ann House was sold to a Mr. Norman Tidwell from Winston County and moved during 1993. Open pasture or farm land located in the cove is privately owned.

Home of Jack McDowell-first Forest Ranger in Bankhead

Narrows Ridge

Narrows Ridge is located in Bankhead Forest in Section 21 of Township 8 South and Range 8 West. While walking south on a ridge from the Northwest Road, suddenly a high narrow strip of land emerges between two beautiful old growth hardwood valleys. The valley to the east was the Borden Creek Canyon and the valley to the west was the Flanagan Creek Canyon. The old settler road along the tip of the ridge continued along the slender natural bridge of sandstone rock connecting the two mountaintop ridges which divided the beautiful creek bottoms. To either side of the old road were the edges of bluffs which rose some 40 to 60 feet above the two hardwood valleys.

The narrow ridge runs in a north-south direction for approximately 100 yards narrowing to as little as some 12 feet wide. The unique and beautiful ridge is known to most local people as the "Narrows Ridge." Narrows Ridge is now in the Addition to the Sipsey Wilderness Area which will provide protection for the beautiful hardwood valleys on either side of this natural ridge.

It appears that early settlers in the area south of Narrows Ridge were also forced to use the connecting strip of rock to get to their valley farms and crops located near the forks of Borden and Flanagan Creeks. The Henderson Family and Parker Family, whose descendants still live in the Moulton area, have roots in the Borden Creek portion of the area. The Gooder Walker family had crops and farm land along the western portion of the area along lower Flanagan Creek.

The road leading to Narrows Ridge is about ¼ mile east of the Mountain Springs Road. The log road runs south from the Northwest Road's highest point between Borden Creek and Flanagin Creek. About 1/2 mile west of Borden Creek, the log road turns south and runs 3/4 mile prior to reaching Narrows Ridge. Narrows Ridge is a unique but beautiful spot in the Black Warrior Mountains.

Needle's Eye

Needles Eye, also known as the Window Rock, is a hole that penetrates the high bluffs that separate Sipsey River from Thompson Creek. This ridge is also known as Herron Point, Boat Rock, or Ship Rock. For a picture of the Needle's Eye, you can see a photo of it under Ship Rock of this section.

Parker Cove

Parker Cove is located in Section 30 of Township 7 South and Range 7 West and is named from the John T. Parker family who settled the cove long ago. Parker Cove forms the headwater streams of Elam Creek on the north-central edge of Bankhead Forest. The cove still contains three old log houses that were used over 100 years ago.

When going south on Highway 33, the main entrance to Parker Cove is along the first steep winding road turning east off of Wren Mountain. The deep cove is visible east of the Wren Mountain portion of the Wilderness Parkway which runs through the center of the Black Warrior Mountains.

Pine Torch Church

The oldest original log church in the State of Alabama is located on the Pine Torch Road in Bankhead Forest in Section 29 of Township 8 South and Range 7 West. The old poplar log church was originally moved from Holmes Chapel, east of

Brushy Lake, and reassembled. The log church is 24 feet wide and 27 feet long, and is over 170 years old.

Pine Torch Church and Cemetery

The first logs were hand hewed in the early 1820s by the Holmes and Nicholson family (1820 Census of Lawrence County). It was originally used for worship services by the congregation known as "Hard-shell Baptists." Blazing pine knots were used to light the church at night. Thus, the church was named Pine Torch. Dr. Charles Borden comments on the protection of the historic Pine Torch Church: "*The Pine Torch Preservation Society, of which I am president, was formed in 1981 to preserve and perpetuate the historical attributes and uses of this memorable part of our heritage.*"

Poplar Log Cove

Poplar Log Cove of the Black Warrior Mountains is located primarily in Section 10 of Township 8 South and Range 6 West. Poplar Log Cove is on the upper portion of the West Fork of Flint Creek in Lawrence County's northeastern portion of Bankhead Forest. Black Warriors' Path traversed through the Cove and passed by the Poplar Log Cove Spring which forms the headwaters of West Flint Creek.

Based on archaeological evidence, Poplar Log Cove was utilized by Indian people as early as the Paleo Period. A Paleo scarper and Decatur Point were found and identified near the center of the cove. Poplar Log Cove was settled in the early 1800s by Indian mixed-bloods and white people. The cove was flat with broad fertile valleys which were farmed in patches of cotton and corn. Today, most of Poplar Log Cove is privately owned but remains one of the most beautiful valleys of the Black Warrior Mountains.

Poplar Springs Cemetery

The Poplar Springs Cemetery is located on the Byler Road in the northwest portion of the Sipsey drainage; the cemetery is the burial site of Jane (Aunt Jenny) Bates Brooks Johnston who was 1/2 Cherokee Indian. Aunt Jenny was born on January 22, 1826, in Walker County and died on March 29, 1924, at the age of 98 at her home near the junction of the Kinlock Road and Byler's Old Turnpike; about one half mile north of Aunt Jenny's home, William McCain, John Byler's son-in-law, operated a toll gate just a few yards south of the forks of the Byler Road and Northwest Road. The Byler Road was made along an Indian trail known as the Old Buffalo Trail; the High Town Path ran a concurrent route with the Old Buffalo Trail to Haleyville where it forked off toward present-day Hodges.

Aunt Jenny had five sons that she claimed all died with their boots on! Aunt Jenny and her first husband Willis Brooks had nine children who were John, Angeline, Mack, Amanda, Willis, Jr., Donna (Donie), Gainam, Henry, and Fanny. For many years, Aunt Jenny served as a midwife for many families who lived on the Byler Road; she out-lived two husbands and all nine of her children.

Quillian Creek

Quillan Creek bears a proper name but was the stomping grounds of the notorious Brooks Boys and Aunt Jenny Brooks Johnson. The creek heads up near the junction of the Byler Road and the Northwest Road and flows southeasterly toward Hubbard Creek; the Quillan Creek bottom is one of the more spectacular scenic walks in the Sipsey Wilderness Area.

Rocky Plains

Those who have never been to the Rocky Plains in the southwest corner of William B. Bankhead Forest may wonder how cottonmouth moccasins and cactus plants can be written about in the same sentence. No two things could be further apart in the natural order of life. What makes it possible for them to be side by side is the lay of the land. They are as separate here as anywhere but the lines that divide them are so narrow that you can step from one to the other.

The area referred to as the Rocky Plains is roughly 30 square miles. One-third of this is low rolling hills of the central plateau with upland hardwood forest. The rest is equally divided between upper coastal plain swamps and rocky pine barrens. The greatest change in the life zones occurs when the rocky pine glades drop directly into the coastal swamps. As far as the snakes are concerned, you can step over the Pygmy Rattlers and cactus to come down on a cottonmouth.

The most remembered thing about the Rocky Plains is the old wagon road that followed the rock shelves across the glade rock. The road, however, is not the oddest thing in the area. On a scale of ten, it would not ever make the ratings, for the Rocky Plains are different, and in many ways strange.

The history of the Plains has changed repeatedly over the years and is still changing, but there is that some intangible thing about them that always seems to remain the same. Maybe it would be best if the story started at the beginning.

Years ago Jim Manasco said, "*Today, we walked the old rocky road across the Plains in the southwest corner of the Bankhead National Forest. The locust buzzed in the trees and the Rain Crow croaked in the woods. Little frogs screamed and jumped into the occasional mud puddle, just as they always have, on our approach and a large lizard ran across the hot rocks dragging a long blue tail.*

Now I was walking the rocky road dragging a long tale also. My dad had walked this road many times just as his father had before him and his before him and his before him. Now 170 years later I was prodding along in their same tracks. I was in the lead and they were behind me for history starts now and run in opposite directions."

It all began about ten thousand years ago in the Ice Age. The ice plugged the Tennessee River and it overflowed down through Alabama. It left in its old path miles of sand and polished gravel down the west side of Winston County (so the County Commissioners would not have to pave any roads). This big washout also left miles of exposed bed rock between Lynn and Poplar Springs. This area is called the Rocky Plains.

The glades and swamps offer the most interesting things to see. The rolling hills are the most common landscape in the state and offer little out of the ordinary. The road that crosses this area follows the dividing line of the watershed. The streams on the east side of the road, Squaw Creek, Doe Branch, Wildcat Branch and Black Creek flow into Clear Creek. The streams on the west side—Browns Creek, Water Creek, Bluff

Creek, and Indian Creek—all flow into Blackwater Creek. The area that these creeks drain in is nearly flat with little fall.

The beavers have found a paradise on the streams in this area. Along the serpentine creeks a foot-high dam can flood 40 acres. Taking advantage of the situation, the beavers have made swamps of every creek and branch on the plains. These swamps have become a haven for wildlife unlike the manmade kind. Here under beaver management all creatures great and small have equal consideration, game species included.

With the studies made to preserve the Sipsey Wilderness Area in the Bankhead National Forest came an abundance of knowledge of both plants and animals in this forest that were before unknown to exist in Alabama. The oddness of this brought many outstanding naturalists to this forest. But what they don't know is that this tiny little corner of the forest, known as the Rocky Plains, has a greater density of wildlife and variety of plants than all the rest of this National Forest combined.

I feel safe in saying that from the beginning of the settlement years, that no more than 70 percent of this area has been walked on by a white man and half of that only once. It is a rough country with few places that are easy to reach and the largest part of the swamps cannot safely be reached at all. It is this absence of man that contributes the most to the variety of animals in this section of the forest.

The fish and game people have come to the swamp and put up many wood duck houses. These houses were placed where the access to the swamps was the easiest. This of course is the place most visited by man and I have not yet seen one in use. The only wood duck nest I know of in the swamp is in a hollow tree deep in the Kaeiser Bottoms. I am not sure what I was doing there when I found it and cannot think of a reason to go back.

The wood ducks should do well here for the swamps are full of all the things they like best and one of those things is a plant called the duck potato. These water-loving plants are also called arrowheads. Botanists are fond of these plants also because of their leaves. The leaves that grow underwater are strap shaped and the ones that grow out of the water are arrowhead shaped. To show their students that the growth control center determines the shaped of the leaf is found in the very tip of the leaf, they make the leaves change places. Fixing the underwater leaves so that the tip is out of the water the plant will grow the arrowhead leaf underwater. By putting the tip of the leaves that grow out of the water into the water makes it grow strap-shaped leaves out of the water.

The wood ducks do not eat the potato of this plant, but do eat the seeds. The root of this plant was a basic food for the Indians where it was available. These duck potatoes also helped the early settlers through some lean times.

It seems that everything on the Rocky Plains is an extreme of one sort or another, from the people to the plants. Down through history the people have had a hard go trying to put down roots in solid rock. Their success had not been very profitable and each year fewer are able to live there. In the last 50 years the decrease in population has been drastic.

The few that live there now have the right idea. Where in the past men tried to live by the rocks today's generation simply live on it; earning their living elsewhere. I suppose that Henry Ford is responsible for that because in the past the old timers had no choice.

This flat rocky plain has been even harder on the plants. Many of them have gone to extremes to survive. The ones that adapted to the situation have done well and the ones that did not wound up in sad shape. The pines that have come up on the plains look different from others on better ground. Finding only enough soil in the cracks to survive they have become stunted with gnarled limbs and twisted trunks. Their silhouette against the sky tells of their hard times on hard rock.

Not all of the plants on the glade rocks have had the troubles the pines did, for they adapted to the rocks. The problem they have now is that they can now live nowhere else. Two of these plants are Rock Portulaca and Cactus. The cactus found its place on the dry rocks and did well. To survive in such a place it converted its leaves to stalks. Leaves use up too much precious water. These it increased in size to serve as water storage compartments for leaner times. The native cactus on the plains lived with the rock rather than by it or on it as man has. It has been here a long time and was food to the Indians before it was a thorn in the white man's foot.

Everyone thinks of the plants of the arid places as being harsh things covered with thorns and stickers. That thought may be almost true, but some of the plants are tender beautiful things. The Rock Potulaca is one of them. This plant only blooms in the heat of the day in the autumn sun. The people that lived around the glades knew this little flower as Sun-Bright, a name that fits it well.

Like the cactus the Sun-Bright converted its leaves to water storage. They are round and spike-like, giving the plant the look of a moss. Its Latin name *Teretifolium* means leaves round in cross sections. The family name *Talinum* was taken from the word thalia, which means green branch. This well describes the plants tender round branch-like leaves. From these leaves the plant sends up wire-like stems and caps each with a lavender flower that is bright as the sun.

Once you have seen the Sun-Bright you get the feeling that this place may not be as harsh as it seems. Knowing this, you can get beyond the harshness and learn to love the place as Chief Richard Brown did before Kaeiser pushed him and his Cherokees off their land.

Saltpeter Well

Saltpeter Well is a glade with a spring in it near Sipsey River just northeast of where the Cullman Motorway crossed the stream. The wells are the trenches dug to collect water used in the manufacture of gunpowder.

You can't tell it now, but the wilderness once was the floor of an ancient sea. The underlying rock base of the wilderness area is fossilized limestone. The limestone can be seen in many places across the wilderness area; two places include the creek bed of Thompson Creek and the river bed of Sipsey River.

This limestone is covered with a cap of sandstone that washed into the sea before the land rose. These rock formations rise from the south on two degrees making the whole of the forest a wedge shaped mountain. While the wilderness is nearly all sandstone, the rest of the forest east of the wilderness is limestone. This limestone is riddled with caves, one having nearly a 100 foot waterfall inside it known as the Devil's Well; the Devil's Well is east of the Mountain Springs Road, south of the Ridge Road, east of Borden Creek, and north of Dement Cemetery.

The cave that is affecting Saltpeter Well is the one on the Northwest Road several miles north of the wilderness. This cave is recorded as Saltpeter Cave and is partly unexplored.

The cave has a stream that runs through it that becomes trapped between the sandstone and limestone and is forced up at Saltpeter Well. As the stream runs through the cave, it dissolves the nitrate from the bat guano and carries it to the wells. The water at the well is undrinkable, but the deer find a tonic value in it and keep the spring worn slick; this is what is called a deer lick.

Saltpeter Well is located near Fall Creek which is the first creek east of the ford where the Old Cullman Motorway crosses the Sipsey River. The easiest way to find it is by walking up the river from the mouth of the creek. There is no problem recognizing it for the supercharged seepage has killed all understory trees that are in the surrounding woods. The spring is surrounded by large trees and the valley is covered with a lush carpet of grass. What has happened here naturally is the same thing that happens when a farmer spreads chicken house fertilizer on his pasture, multiplied by a hundred.

The ridge that the old Cullman Motorway Road goes up by the wells is of very soft sandstone filled with gravel and fossils of plants. This ridge on its west face has exposure of this stone. The stone, being what it is, weathers faster than the sandstone in the rest of the wilderness. This stone is full of potholes and weathers in strange shapes. This allows seeds to germinate in the rocks themselves and produces a strange array of serpentine roots of the trees that grow on the large boulders.

This unusual geological occurrence has been a windfall to one rare species of wild flowers. The round leafed catchfly over the years has adapted to grow only in the cracks of sandstone bluffs. Due to the scarcity of sandstone bluffs, it has a limited existence. Yet here on the face of these rocks with their countless weathered holes it has found a habitat unequaled. The pale green foliage drapes from the sockets in the rocks like the vines of a nurseryman's hanging basket. The blooms are a vivid red-orange and last from late May through December.

This plant has a sticky substance that coats the stems and leaves. Any insect that walks on them are trapped. This gives the plant its common name of catchfly. Its botanical name is *Silene rotundafolia*. This plant is camera shy, when photographed with black and white film the green of the leaves on the pale gray of the rocks disappear. The blooms come out black and the end picture is a picture of a rock. When photographed in color, however, it looks like orange and lime sherbet.

Saltpeter Wells is a strange and different kind of place in the Sipsey Wilderness, but you will never find it without the Bee Branch Quadrangle Map.

Ship Rock

Ship Rock is located in the Sipsey Wilderness Area in Section 27 of Township 8 South and Range 9 West. The large rock is located some 200 yards east of the forks of Hubbard and Thompson Creeks in the heart of the Sipsey Wilderness. The site is known as Ship Rock, Herron Point, Boat Rock, Needle's Eye, or the Windows.

The following text is a descriptive but symbolic version of the Ship Rock of Sipsey. The mighty Ship Rock of the Black Warrior is sailing east dragging the mountains and canyons of unspeakable beauty through the universe. In front of her awesome sandstone bow is the Tugboat Rock of the forest leading the way and breaking the bonds of time to allow the Ship Rock to meet her destiny beyond the knowledge of humankind. The Tugboat Rock is always at her bow never allowing her voyage to be slowed by the forces of time.

Needle's Eye with my daughters at its base

Near the stern of tugboat rock is the Needle's Eye which focuses the last easterly flowing rays caught from the westerly setting sun to provide the brief sailing light toward the east before darkness again dims the mighty ship's journey. Thousands of years ago, the forces of time blasted the hole called the Windows or Needle's Eye at the stern of Tugboat Rock yet, undaunted, the little sandstone tug maintains a true course guiding the mighty Ship Rock through the earth's celestial sphere.

Out of Hubbard Creek Canyon, and through the middle of King Cove, she sails leaving a deep botanical trough and solid standing waves of sandstone which begin to close at the falling waters of Parker, Quillan, and Kinlock. The waterfalls of the Black Warrior Mountains send the melodious sound waves of the true wilderness lapping at her sides. At the bow of Ship Rock, the crest rises high, creating vast depressions of beautiful valleys through which the Sipsey and Thompson waters

136

flow. Forever eastward toward the rising sun, dawns a new day for her forested sea. She plows and pulls the high bluffs as she churns constantly through the land of a thousand waterfalls. From the botanical gardens of the limestone valleys, to the hardwood ridges of the sandstone slopes, she has sailed from before the time of the dinosaurs toward eternity with the timeless canyons of the Black Warrior Mountains lashed firmly to her stern.

Ship Rock has a great deck nearly 1,000 feet in length and over 100 feet wide. Her bow is a sharp rising crest which rides high in the waves of the air reaching nearly 60 feet above first contact with her timbered and stony sea. Her stern is broad with the great force of Mother Nature driving her through the mountainous sea, always leaving the beginning of Sipsey in her wake. Her sides, adorned with big flowered trillium, Virginia bluebells, blue cohosh, and Dutchman's breeches, rise some 50 feet to the mountain laurel and Vir-

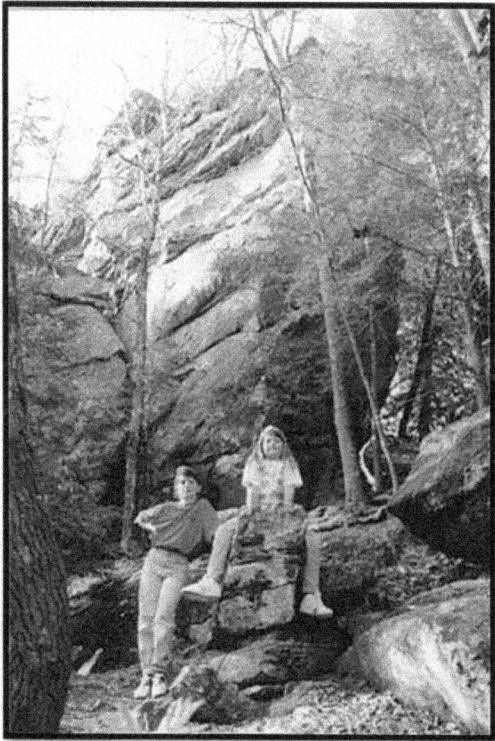

Ship Rock's massive bow 80 ft above canyon floor

137

ginia pine covered deck.

Ship Rock is a monument in time and a symbol of persistence before the age of the great reptilian dinosaurs, the age of the gigantic mammals, and the age of the red man who once inhabited her great forested seas. No time, force, or age is her master, for God is her pilot and only he knows her true destiny. As God spins the eternal swirl of the universe, Ship Rock holds steady while dragging the Black Warrior Mountains along with the rest of the world.

Where are the huge Ship Rock, the Tugboat Rock, and the Needle's Eye? These geologic wonders are woven into the fabric of Lawrence County's Black Warrior Mountains. The magnificent weaver left his Needle's Eye as a guide for those who may think they are lost to the great ship and the little tug.

Now for directions: From the Byler Road, turn east on the Northwest Road and go to the dead end at Thompson Creek Bridge. Take the wilderness trail which turns south down the east side of the beautiful Thompson Creek Canyon. You will hike about one and a half hours before you see a large hole in the face of the bluff just prior to reaching the forks of Thompson and Hubbard Creeks. You have arrived at the Ship Rock of the Black Warrior Mountains.

Sipsey River

Today canoes are seen regularly on the Sipsey River. In search of the wild, people will launch their boats and, mustering all their strength, paddle as fast as they can through the wilderness. This is not the way the old timers did it.

River camping is old to the Sipsey. People have been doing it since aboriginal times and white settlers during the horse and buggy days. Camping was different then, the woods were wilder and the people were in no hurry. Where the roads would allow, they camped under the bluffs near the river. It was family camping and a chance to visit with seldom seen friends.

Some of the men that knew the forest in those days felt that this type of camping was too civilized and headed for the deep woods that were all but inaccessible. I have, in the past, had the privilege of going with those grand old men of the forest on a few of their fishing trips.

The manner in which they went camping would astonish today's campers. They appeared to be carrying nothing. As for food, the contents of a half-filled feed sack would be sufficient for six men for several days. It contained salt, lard, meal and coffee. One man carried the sack, another an ax, and the rest carried nothing that could be seen. When they reached their destination, they would set up camp under a bluff. Eating nothing but fish until they, as they put it, "*got a bait of it.*"

A little before dark someone would cut two sticks and a minnow seine would mysteriously appear. Going to the rapids, a biscuit would be placed underwater with a rock on top of it. The bread floating downstream would attract minnows which were then caught for bait. No boat was needed; they just rocked up a pool in the river and waded the lines out. During the night, the lines would be run several times and rebaited. There was never a shortage of fish. A man could stay forever if he could stand the diet. They normally stayed about five or six days.

There was one man that went to the Sipsey River and

stayed. He was a true hermit. There were two more, other than him, which I refer to as semi-hermits in that they did not completely break all ties with the human race.

The true hermit was called Goat Man. One of the other two was also called by that name and lived on the river below the Recreation Area in a house and many knew him. He was sociable and not wild like the other. As long as I can remember, the old mountain men talked of the hermit. It was some sort of a game with them to track him and try to figure out what he had been doing. None of them had ever seen him and addressed him as the wildest thing in the woods.

In the late 1950s, I was spending a lot of time in the Riddles Fields area and became aware of his presence there. He seemed to have set up residence in that area in a secluded cove. I knew he was there and went to great lengths to avoid his territory because I felt it was his.

In 1961, I was spending some time just walking around in that area when he suddenly appeared in a clearing. A sadder sight one could not imagine. His clothes were several layers thick and literally torn to shreds. His long hair and beard looked blond but I think it was dirt in gray. He looked at me and left in a straight line through the woods making no attempt to hide his trail.

I look back on that day and curse my own ignorance. He was making contact with me the only way he knew how and I did not have the gumption to realize it. After two years without seeing any sign of him, I followed the trail that he had wanted me to follow that day; it went straight to his camp. No one has seen any sign of him lately and I am sure he is dead. He was a complete success; he lived just as he wanted to without anyone telling him anything. He went to the Sipsey and remained there.

I met another semi-hermit on one of my lone ranger fishing trips in the forest once. I was catching spot tail minnows on worms and using them for bass bait on green cane poles. I kept losing them because of the limber poles. I was being watched.

Presently a young man came down and talked with me for a while. He was living in a cave hiding from the law. After a while, I told him I had to go and he said that I could not go without some fish. He went to a branch nearby and flipped over a few rocks coming back with five salamanders.

> I guess one fish hook can be mighty important when you are alone in the woods.

Taking a line and hook from his pocket, he dropped it over the side of the rock we were sitting on and pulled up five catfish as fast as he could bait the hook. He gave me the fish and smilingly said that there was a cave under the rock that was always full of catfish. He said that he once swam in it and almost did not get out. I guess one fish hook can be mighty important when you are alone in the woods.

The river has not changed since those days; it is the people that have changed. There are as many fish in the river as ever and if you could slow down your shiny new canoe you may find them.

South Caney Creek

South Caney Creek has two of the most spectacular waterfalls in the Bankhead Forest; there is an upper falls which is as far as most people hike and a lower falls that is just as beautiful as the upper. North and South Caney Creeks lie between the Cranal Road which some people call the Sipsey River Picnic

Grounds Road and the County Highway 2 that runs west from Highway 33 to Highway 195; Highway 195 connects Haleyville and Double Springs.

To get to South Caney Creek Falls, you need to go west from Highway 33 on County Road 2 to the forest service gate some four to five miles. From the gate on County Highway 2, the upper falls are about a mile and the lower falls is prior to reaching the junction of North and South Caney Creeks.

Tar Springs Hollow

Tar Springs Hollow is located in the upper portion of Capsey Creek, once known as Capp's Creek; the creek canyon is a place not found elsewhere in William B. Bankhead National Forest. The creek begins at Cave Springs on Highway 41 just south of the junction of the Leola Road. West a few miles along the Leola Road is Basham Shelter and Spring. The area, not noted for the two head water springs, is unique because of the two springs downstream in the middle of the big hollow. This unusual site found on Capsey Creek is known as Tar Springs Hollow.

Capsey Creek is a tributary to Brushy Creek which empties its waters into Sipsey River on Smith Lake. The Tar Springs Hollow on Capsey Creek contains two mineral tar springs which are located about once quarter mile apart in the southwest 1/4 of Section 26, Township 8 South, and Range 6 West.

According to the Alabama Geological Survey as reported by geologist Jonathan Hunter and made available by Mr. Leon Hightower, "*These springs years ago were places of a resort for the afflicted who drank their waters and swallowed their tar or maltha, made into pills, and supposed that they were greatly benefitted thereby. The hotel and cottages for the accommoda-*

tions of the visitors to these springs are said to have stood on the hill just south of this lower spring. Both of these springs, however, have been spoiled by blasting them for asphaltum."

The article also indicated that barrels of tar were collected in holes made in the floor of the springs and shipped off. In addition to the Tar Springs, oil wells were drilled in 1865 and 1867 that were between 700 and 800 feet deep. The geological survey reports that Jonathan Watson probably drilled and got oil out of the wells in Tar Springs Hollow.

According to material furnished by Mr. Rayford Hyatt, the Tar Springs Hollow Road was one route many settlers and visitors took to the Tar Springs Resort. The early road led from Melton's Bluff to Oakville, then to Poplar Log Cove where the road forked. The eastern fork in Poplar Log Cove was the main route of the Black Warriors' Path or Mitchell Trace; on December 19 1835, Creek Chief Opoth-leyaholo (Laughing Fox) and 511 Creek people followed the Mitchell Trace through Poplar Log Cove to the Coo-sa Path at Oakville where they turned west toward Tus-cumbia Landing.

The south fork

Opothleyaholo (Laughing Fox)
1778-3/22/1863

143

became known as the Tar Springs Hollow Road or Double Springs Road and traveled south up Wiggins Hollow and passed the old Asherbranner Cemetery. The road crossed the High Town Path east of Center Church and passed down a long ridge into Tar Springs Hollow.

From the 1800s through the early 1900s, prior to the National Forest status the land has today, many people lived in the area of Tar Springs Hollow. Cave Springs Cemetery and Center Cemetery contain the remains of many who called the Tar Springs Hollow area home. It appears from examinations of the tombstones in Cave Springs and Center Cemetery, that many of the people were descendants of the Creek and Cherokee Indians, the earlier inhabitants of the area.

Many of the family names of those who presently compose the Lawrence County Indian population are found in the old cemeteries. The family names at Center Cemetery include Osborn, Smith, Williams, McVay, Hampton, Jackson, Steele, Holley, Looney, Wood, Eddy, Asherbranner, Poole, Burnett, Hogan, Rooks, Kelsoe, Johnson, Cooper, and many others. These mixed-blood Celtic Indian family names still persist in the southeastern part of Lawrence County.

In the area of Tar Springs, the forest seemed eternal except for the destructive clear cutting activity. In the late evening as the eerie sounds of a screech owl were emerging from the forest, it was hard for me to imagine how the area might have looked when the hotel and cottages within the rugged canyon were alive with people seeking the healing powers of the Tar Springs in the heart of the Black Warrior Mountains.

Thompson Creek

Thompson Creek is bound to have been named for someone

associated with the creek. The families that lived there were named Peoples, Riddles, Spillers, Beavers, Garrisons, and many others. The first mile of the trail will take you to White Oak Hollow; at the junction of White Oak Branch and Thompson Creek was Beavers Sawmill. Just a short distance from Thompson on the south side of White Oak Branch is a huge American beech tree with the initials of James Calvin Riddle and Amos Spillers dated 1918; James and

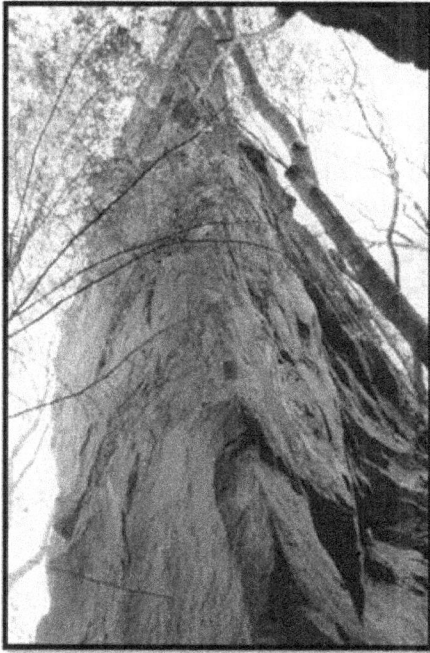

Bow of Ship Rock

Amos were mixed-blood Cherokees.

A trail leads downstream along the east side where Northwest Road crosses Thompson Creek Bridge; the trailhead starts on the southeast side of the bridge. The trail leads to Ship Rock, Bee Branch, and many other points of interest. The path is many miles long and loops deep through the wilderness and comes out on the mountain above Bee Branch where it forks to the southeast along the old Bunyan Hill Road to the Borden Creek Trailhead; the northwest fork turns up the old Bunyan Hill Road and leads to the trailhead near Gum Pond Cemetery off the Braziel Creek Road. Where the Bunyan Hill Road intersects the closed portion of the Northwest Road, another trail leads west along the North-

145

west Road back to the Thompson Creek Trailhead.

Ugly Creek

Ugly Creek is not ugly unless you compare it to Parker Branch. Compared to Parker Branch, every creek in the wilderness would be ugly. None of the branches that make up this creek have names, but they have some of the most beautiful waterfalls in the Sipsey Wilderness Area.

White Oak Hollow

White Oak Hollow is named for the most numerous species of trees in the forest; hickory is the second most numerous tree in the natural forest. In the mouth of White Oak Hollow, a beech tree has the name of James Calvin Riddle and Amos Spillers; both of the men are of mixed-blood Cherokee Indian ancestry and were brother-in-laws at one time. The tree carving has J. C. Riddle on one line; the next line is the date 1918; and, Amos makes up the third line. They worked at Beaver's Sawmill which was in the mouth of White Oak Hollow on Thompson Creek.

Wolf Pen

Wolf Pen Branch heads up at the cemetery of the same name and flows north into the Sipsey River. Wolf Pen Cemetery was once the site of an old log school. The name comes from some sort of trap that was used to catch wolves in the early white settlement days.

The Bankhead National Forest belongs to you. Use it wisely and insist that the forest service does the same. If you do drive the roads in the forest, you are likely to see things that have happened that you don't like.

FLORA AND FAUNA OF SIPSEY

Beech Trees with Southern Marks

In the wilderness, as everywhere else in the South, men have been drawn to the creek bottoms, whether to fish, swim, or live there. They came and left their mark.

Here along the creek banks are those big trees with their massive trunks and smooth bark that attracted them to leave a sign. A habit of man has left a written history of his presence in the deep woods.

The oldest part of any trees is the outer bark. As the tree grows, any mark placed on it remains and becomes larger as the tree ages. Because Beech Trees are long-lived, some of the marks on them can be two or three hundred years old and still be visible. The Indians called these trees boundary trees and placed signs on them marking tribal grounds. They used them for other signs also and many of the signs on the old ones are of Indian origin. Things like birds, snakes, circles, triangles, dots and lines mark the trees.

No beech tree in our time should be cut or defaced because of the history recorded on them. It would be like burning a book. These trees often bare a written legacy of man's history in the South with a record on the trees and nowhere else. The most common mark placed on beech trees was the "X" which is the mark of a bee tree. The early settlers did not often keep bees, but furnished the table with honey. The hollows in beech trees were perfect hives for the wild bees.

When the settlers would find a bee at its watering place, they would watch the bee leave flying straight to his hive.

DOUBLE MARKED BEE TREE

Coursing the bee along the bee line is hard to do through the woods. So they would try to trap a bee at the water and attach a fluff of cotton to him so they could see him easier.

Once the tree was found, the man would place an "X" on it so his neighbors would know that it was his tree; one he would rob at a later time. Each man would have a different way of marking his tree so others would know who he was. Some would write his name by the "X", others would place another mark by it, such as an arrow, line, or something of that nature. Others were recognized by the size of the "X" or the number of them.

The number of different kinds of signs in a confined area is determined by how many families live there. The largest variety of bee tree marks in the wilderness is found along Thompson Creek. Two of those signs pictured in this section are Joe's tree on the Thompson Creek Trail and the double sign tree up White Oak Branch.

The beech trees throughout the wilderness are a variable source of written history. They have the names and dates of the first settlers, the names and dates of the first survivors of the land, and the names and dates of the Forest Service people that were walking the lines when the National Forest was in its formative years.

Though I have not seen one, I am sure the Indian signs are there. The Indians also left signs on these beech trees. The trees are not the only things here they put a sign on.

After all those years of wandering the forest, it never occurred to me of the history cut in beech trees until recently I noticed the variation of bee tree signs. Looking for these signs has brought forth a wealth of unexpected information in the wilderness.

What started here has since carried me out of the forest to other places. It was reasonable that if the early settlers left the marks here they did it everywhere.

Recently walking down the hollow behind my wife's old home place, on the first beech tree, I found the names and dates of her brothers placed there many years ago.

If you know where your grandparents lived, then go there and look at the beech trees, for they may have left you a message. It is a delightful way to enjoy the woods and, at times when you least expect it, most rewarding.

If you yearn for something older than your roots, then go to the Jasper Library and look at a book called *The Cry of the Eagles*. This book has pictures of Cherokee trees sign in north Georgia. While the signs around here are of a different tribe, they are still quite similar.

Beech trees have furnished us with a form of outdoor recreation that is available to all without the study that is necessary with the natural history associated with wilderness and can be enjoyed anywhere, even the creeks in town.

Flowers of Thompson Creek

The continental United States is divided into three major frost zones. These zones are established by the dates of the last frost. On Thompson Creek, the northern and southern zones overlap, splitting the central zone. Here on this part of the forest is the only place that this happens. The valley here is also seven degrees warmer than the ridge above in the winter and seven degrees cooler in the summer. To predict when something will blossom here is not possible. It changes every year.

A short hike down the trail and then back out the same way will treat you to an array of native wildflowers. The only way you can predict what flowers will bloom a week in advance is to go look a week before for the ones still in bud. Wildflowers do not last as long as the cultivated varieties, so if you go to the same place once a week you will see a different set. The wildflowers that you will see along the trail are as follows:

Trillium: Several species will be blooming including the dark red twisted petal and the Big Whites. Trilliums get their names from having three of everything: three leaves, three sepals, and three petals.

May Apples: It is interesting to note that only the plants with forked stems will bloom.

Jack in Pulpit: The jack is the spadix and the spathe folds over to form the pulpit. You cannot see the flower, it is hidden in the bottom of the pulpit.

Showy Orchids: Surprised? Alabama has many native wild orchids.

Red Buckeye: These buckeyes never reach tree size and are the ones that grow the Lucky Buckeyes.

Pawpaw: Most everyone knows what a pawpaw looks like but how many would recognize the bloom?

PAWPAW IN BLOOM IN EARLY SPRING

Doll's Eyes: The flowers are not as showy as the seeds. This fall these blooms will look like a cluster of grapes growing upside down. The grapes will be white and each will have a black dot on it. The vine part will be bright red. They are as poisonous as they are colorful.

Wild Geraniums, White Larkspurs, and Blue Phlox will line the trail as you walk down the stream.

Moving off the trail to the bluff, the big moss-covered rocks are hanging gardens of ginger and ferns.

The above listings of wildflowers are only a small sample of all the varieties of flowering plants in view on your hike. Take time to behold the beauty of the wildflower array as you walk the Thompson Creek Trail.

Do not pick the flowers or you may have to pay!

Ferns Older Than Trees

Surviving from older times, the non-flowering plants are the oldest things in the forest today. Here in the Sipsey Wilderness Area, we have nearly a hundred species of ferns. The county with the most is probably Winston. This places the Wilderness area as the number one fern spot in the state. Ferns are found here in abundance in all areas. The variation of the land mass of the Wilderness is the main factor in the diversity of species. The hill tops, creek beds, bluffs, and valleys each have different kinds of ferns.

There is a lot of fact and fiction concerning ferns. It was believed in old days that placing the spores of the ferns in your shoes would make you invisible. Shakespeare mentioned this in Henry IV when he wrote, "We have receipt of fern seed, we walk invisible." Of course that is absurd, but people are not much wiser about ferns today.

One fact about ferns is that the spores are explosive; they were used for the flash by the old photographers. This explosive nature may have something to do with the Bracken Ferns that grow in profusion after the woods burn.

Ferns are very nice around the house and do well in flower gardens. They transplant easily and thrive when placed in a new location comparable to the one they were moved from. With the increase in surface mining, you could do yourself and the ferns a favor by rescuing them. As the ferns have been here the longest, they have had more time to adapt than the other plants. This is very evident in the way they grow in the wilderness.

Rattlesnake Ferns grow on the hill sides where the water will drain away from the roots, under the hardwood trees.

Broad Leaf Beech Ferns are found mostly under beech trees; over the years the fern and the trees have formed some sort of a binding relationship.

Dryopteris Wood Ferns have a habit of growing between the big rocks that have rolled off the mountains into the valleys.

Cinnamon and Royal Ferns grow in the spring runs and branches where they can keep their feet wet.

Goldinana Ferns live in the upper margins of the flood plains along the creeks. They are very rare, large, and pretty.

Northern Maidenhair Ferns are found in most depressions in the deep woods where their fragile stems are protected.

Lobed Spleenworts grow only in the dry cracks on the fractures of sandstone bluffs.

Ebony Stemmed Spleenworts have a habit of growing on old rock piles around tumbled-down houses.

It is easy to see that each fern has its own place in the forest and they never seem to compete for the same piece of ground as the trees and other plants. In fact, two ferns have adapted to places that little if anything would compete for.

Filmy Ferns only grow hanging from the ceilings of the rock shelters where the sun never shines. They have adapted to the point that they are only one cell thick so that they can survive on very little light.

Peters Fern is also one cell thick and grows almost in the dark, but has done the filmy fern one better. It has to be constantly misted with water, so it only grows behind waterfalls.

Both of these ferns have so adapted that they can live nowhere else. If the trees in front of the bluffs are cut and the strong light comes in, the filmy fern dies. If the water flow is interrupted, the Peters Fern dies.

Yet it is obvious that the **Christmas Ferns** have not adapted to any condition and are found most everywhere. The teacher tells me that adaption of the species leads to the survival of the fittest. The ferns tell me that adaption leads to extinction.

Christmas Ferns, Norwegian rats, flies, and pine trees that live and grow everywhere, being adapted to little or nothing, seem to be in no danger. It is the things that become so set in their ways that they cannot or will not change their ways that get run over and wiped out.

February—Time for Tree Frogs

Soon it will be time for the tree frogs to migrate. After their long winter sleep in the woods, they will start to migrate back to the breeding ponds. February's first warm rain sets things moving. At this time, a drive through un-reclaimed strip pits will give you a ringside seat to the annual frog migration.

The wild creatures come out for the migration also. The little screech owl's favorite dish is frog, which he catches while they are in the road and easy to get to; raccoons have never been known to turn them down, either.

There is nothing quite so pleasing as the sound of tree frogs on a summer night, and now is the time to stock up. They are easy to pick up under the headlights. A gallon milk jug with a flap cut at the top makes a perfect container.

Release the frogs in a wet place or pond around the house and they will sing for you all summer. A word of caution: The pickerel frog is poison. His skin secretes a fluid that is very irritating.

Soon the ditches will be ringing with the sound of summer frogs. One of these is the spring peeper. This small gray tree frog has a black cross on his back. He does not have the ability to change his color the way the green tree frog does.

The green tree frog is the one the old timers call the rain frog because he has a way of singing the most just before the summer rains. That is not just a tale; he really does. What could possibly sense moisture in the air better than a frog? So if you want to see a frog migration, the time is at hand.

Ruth Manasco found this out when the green tree frog she was photographing zapped a bystander dead center. It pays to be ready.

Way Down in the Pawpaw Patch

A man that would eat a pawpaw would eat nearly anything. Pawpaws have been sold on the market, but then so has nearly everything else. In a smelling or tasting contest, there are few things below a pawpaw.

So the question arises, "Just what is Susie going to do with all those pawpaws she was putting in her basket?"

One authority on the subject says that pawpaws have two different kinds of fruit. Had he been better versed, he would have known that there are three different species in Alabama.

The country folks say there are only two kinds: the tall bush and the low bush. The tall bush is the one in the song.

The other two, dwarf and dog apples, are called low bush.

It is true that tall bush pawpaws do grow in patches along stream banks around here. The other two knee-high varieties don't; they just mix in with everything else.

The fruit on all of them is about the same. When it is ripe it emits an odor not as repulsive as the taste. This fruit will spoil almost on touch. Putting it in a basket would be disastrous, getting it to market impossible.

So just what does the pawpaw have that is worth singing about? It is no good for lumber and not pretty enough to be planted.

It does have one characteristic that some might consider worthwhile. The fruit of the pawpaw, be it bruised, spoiled, or in the basket, can be made into a spirituous liquor.

Maybe Susie knows more than she's telling. Maybe that is why so many people are looking for her.

Bloodroot Tied to State History

All men are victims of their society. We are taught from the time of birth there is little value but money value, little truth but scientific truth. So when someone shows us a bloodroot we can neither sell nor eat, our minds go blank.

Of all the little plants that grow around us, none is more directly tied to our history than this one. A little knowledge of it is very rewarding. When white men first came to this part of the state they found Indians living along the streams. So they called them Creeks. Another name for them was the "Red Sticks," because they had a system by which their towns voted in troubled times.

A stick was passed from town to town. Each town was allotted a portion of that stick. If the town voted for action, it painted its part red. If the stick returned to the original town painted totally red, the Creeks were united in a declaration of war.

BLOODROOT

The paint for the stick was made from the bloodroot. This root, when crushed, furnished a vivid red permanent dye that was used for many things, for painting the stick the least.

To my knowledge the red stick was only used in modern times over white man's abuse of the land.

The French sure felt the sting of this red stick. The survivors fled Fort Toulouse never to forget this "Baton Rouge," which is French for "red stick."

The Creeks are gone from our hills now but the bloodroot is still here. The Indians were just not mean enough to survive.

They saw the trees on the mountains silhouetted against the sky and said, "the mountains and the trees are forever, only the people shall pass away." I looked yesterday and the trees were gone. I looked today and the mountain was gone.

History has a way of repeating itself and land use is still a problem. As governments go, the Indian had little or none and some think we have one too big and too much.

And all think that government should have all the answers. But governments are not supposed to be smart, governments only govern. They cannot legislate knowledge, they can only regulate ignorance. I guess how big or little they are is determined by the size of what they are regulating.

Northern Birds in Sipsey

January is a good month to be a bird. They don't feel the cold the way we do. The fluffs on the inside of their feathers serve as air traps to hold body heat. The only parts of a bird that are exposed to the elements are the feet and beak. These are nothing but sinew and bone and are not subject to cold.

Many birds come to North Alabama to spend the winter. They come not because of the cold but rather because of food. The snows of the north cover their seeds and force them to fly south.

The only thing important to a bird is food.

I remember when the Cedar Wax Wing came here by the thousands. In those days there were hedges in every yard. It was a fad to plant them along walks and trim them into unnatural shapes. These privets were an imported species and as long as people kept planting them they would spread. Many people planted them in hedge rows that were never trimmed. These were covered in the late fall and winter with dark blue berries. The wax wings loved them. They would so cover these bushes that they would fold under their weight.

These hedges furnished these birds with an abundant food

supply. Now that the hedges are dying off the number of Wax Wings is also being reduced. Yet today there are likely more of these birds than ever before. They are a bird of open fields and broken forest. As all of America was once virgin forest not nearly so many could have survived.

January is the month of the snowbird. These little slate grey birds are called Juncos. They come to this area in numbers in the winter. They flock with other birds that are also here for the winter. You see them often with Purple Finches. These birds look like sparrows that have had red paint splattered on them.

This time of year I am always amazed by the Goldfinches. This time of year they are drab green with just a hint of yellow. Yet in six weeks they will be a brilliant yellow with black wings. This sudden change will occur seemingly overnight.

There is another bird that shows up this time of year that is the same color of a Goldfinch but he is as large as a Blue Jay. This bird is the Evening Grosbeak. They generally come in flocks and are very noisy.

While some of the winter birds may be more interesting to see, I am still partial to the ones that stay here year-round. I like the Chickadees. The black mask and cap completely hide their eyes. They always seem to be doing something of the utmost importance, though I am not sure what and suspect they are not sure either.

They have a very pleasing song in the early spring. It is a song that is so much a part of spring that few people ever realize they hear it. They have a habit of hanging out with Titmice, which are the most common bird around. Everyone has seen Titmice, or mouse singular, but no one seems to know them by name. They just call them birds, or at best little birds.

When the cold weather comes and it is too uncomfortable

to spend time outdoors, it is nice to have a bird feeder outside the window. You can get close to them, and all book stores have books that will identify them on a feeder. One would never suspect the number of different kinds that live in their yards. Birds that have been there all along, but have never been seen.

The best food to put on a feeder is sunflower seeds. If you put out some of the smaller seed you will also get some of the field birds like a number of the small field sparrows. If you want to go all the way, wrap some fat meat in wire and hang it on a tree; it will attract the woodpeckers. This will keep you busy all winter just trying to identify them.

It is always surprising how many people know the names of birds, but do not know them when they see them. Birds like the Rain Crow, Sapsucker, Bee Martins, Red Breasted Woodpeckers, Fly Catchers, Tanagers, Warblers, and many more. There is a big world out there and a lot of it is in your yard. Knowledge of it is very satisfying.

Ginseng: Fact and Fantasy

Without question, the most sought after, universally known, talked about, and mysterious plant on earth is ginseng.

It has been known and used by man for probably 10,000 years. It has been historically recorded for almost 5,000.

In recent times, a system has been devised to name plants so they could be known by the same name worldwide. The botanical name for ginseng is *Panax quinquefolius.*

There is a lot to a name. The word panax is the family name for all different kinds of ginseng. The word is from two other words: "pan" which is "all" and "ak os" which is "remedy." The species name of quinquefolius is "quinque," for five, and "folius," for foliated. When you say *Panax quinquefolius* you are saying five-leafed cure-all.

You can go anywhere in the world and use this name and anyone acquainted with this plant will know you are talking about American ginseng.

There are several different kinds of ginseng and no two have the same last name. There are two kinds here in the south. The other is *Panax trifolius*, or three-leaved ginseng.

The common name ginseng is a corruption of the highly-prized Manchurian species which is *Panax schinseng*. This variety has large roots in the shape of a man's body from the neck down. A single root from this species has sold for as much as $500.

Common names are not very hard to identify with; here in the South, ginseng is known as: American ginseng, dwarf ginseng, dwarf groundnut, five fingers, garatogen, ginseng, graentiquere, jinsard, man's health, manroot, ninsin, redberry, sang, and tartar root.

Many of the things we have heard about ginseng are true and some are not. The Chinese say that flowers of this plant glow in the dark, but if a man comes near the light goes out. So they would go in the night and look for this light and shoot arrows at it. When day came they would look for the arrows to find the ginseng. Since ginseng grows in the same places that glowworms live, they may have been shooting at the worms and finding the ginseng.

It has been found, in recent years, that the ground on which it grows and the plant itself are slightly radioactive. But, then again, so is an onion. There are several plants that glow in the dark, but I do not believe that ginseng is one of them.

Many of the things we have heard about ginseng since Americans started digging it in the 1600s here in the US are true. Most of the doubt has been brought about because we are a new nation with no ties to the past.

All drugs are derived from nature. Some of these are man-ufactured artificially to reduce cost. Eighty percent of all drugs sold in a drugstore cannot be explained scientifically as to why they work. We know that they do only because of trial and error and longtime use. Science has no notion why an aspirin will stop pain.

Yet Americans doubt that ginseng is of any medical value. While researching for this paper, it has become apparent to me that untold millions of people have used this medicine for thou-sands of years; I cannot conceive that many people could be that wrong for that long. This is where medicine comes from.

The history of ginseng is available to the world and while this country has been scoffing at ginseng, others have been studying it. England, Germany, Russia, South Korea, Japan, and a half dozen other countries have been conducting studies of the plant.

Chemical analysis of the plant shows that the plant con-tains saponins that are medically active, along with vitamins and minerals. These give a person strength and health and re-sistance to stress. It has been found that ginseng has a rejuve-nating quality and increases mental ability. All this combined can lengthen life.

In China, ginseng was dug to the point of extinction. The government made it a crime to dig it. Ginseng then became the first endangered species by the action of man and the first to be protected by law.

This caused the Chinese to have to go outside their nation to obtain it. So "sang" hunters came to America on the heels of Columbus.

The American ginseng is not considered as strong as the Asian varieties but the amount made up the difference. It was shipped from America by the ton.

After 400 years of continual commercial digging in the United States, ginseng is in trouble. The only thing that the American cared about was how much money they could make digging it—about $80 a pound.

What most people don't realize is how much you have to dig to get a pound. The roots of our ginseng are small. Before they can be sold, they must be washed and dried, leaving them weighing about as much as a peanut in the shell. It takes so much walking, searching, and preparation that it is hardly worth the price. Have you ever seen a rich sang hunter?

In this and other countries, men have tried to grow ginseng commercially and all have failed. It takes the seed two years to come up and the root from five to seven years to mature. The wild kind is about all there is.

In the hill country of Alabama, ginseng grows in the damp hollows among the rocks. It hides under other plants along the spring runs, where no man treads. It is as dark and mysterious as it ever was.

It would be sad if we lost this species just as we were starting to learn something about it. It is still being dug and is in a state of serious decline.

The endangered status of this plant has caused the government to close all export of the roots in an effort to stop the decline. If this does not occur, the plant protection, it will be placed on the federal register and like in China, it will be a crime to dig it.

What most men don't know is that every effort is made to keep species off the federal register. It is used only when all else fails.

It's like the snail darter. They knew it was there before they started the project and started anyway. It has to stop somewhere.

Every time we lose a species, our quality of life is reduced. It is estimated that 20 percent of all the species will be extinct in the near future, and no one can profit from that.

We worry too much about our dead and give no consideration to those yet unborn.

Ginseng: It's OK to Look but Don't Touch

Ginseng hunters are still active in the Sipsey Wilderness of the Black Warrior Mountains. They roam the hills digging the herb with little thought or ceremony. The reason it is still a market item is the same as it was a thousand years ago, but the manner in which is dug is quite different.

In the old days the only medicine was that which was found in the woods. They believed that God had marked all plants with a sign showing what they would cure. Plants with heart shaped leaves were for heart medicine, foot shaped for the foot and the like were the doctrines of signatures.

The ginseng plant had a root shaped like a man's body and was used by men having problems with their manhood. This gave the plant its old name of Mandrake.

AMERICAN GINSENG - BRAZIEL CREEK

The plants that were marked had spirits and had to be approached in certain manners. Many of the common names of plants today have origins from those days. They are ended with the word "wort" like spiderworts, St. Johnsworts, and Louseworts.

Ginseng had a very strong spirit and it was really bad for the fellow who touched it. So in the year 1484, Apuleii Platonici wrote a book of instructions on how the plant was to be dug. That book is now some 524 years old and it reads as follows…

"Thou shalt in this manner take it, when thou comest to it, then thou understandest it by this, that it shineth at night altogether like a lamp. When first thou seest its head, then inscribe thou it instantly with iron, left it fly from thee; its virtue is so mickle and famous, that it will immediately flee from an unclean man, when he cometh to it; hence as we before said, do thou inscribe (encircle) it with iron, and so shalt thou delve about it, as that thou touch it not with the iron, but thou shalt earnestly with an ivory staff delve the earth. And when thou seest its hands and its feet, then tie it up. Then take the earth end and tie it to a dog's neck, so that the hound be hungry; next cast meat before him, so that he may not reach it, except he jerk up the wort with him. Of this wort it is said, that it is has no mickle might, then that thing soever tuggeth it up, that it shall soon in the same manner be deceived. Therefore as soon as thou see that it be jerked up, and have possession of it, take it immediately in hand, and twist it, and wring the ooze out of its leaves into glass ampulla."

It is hard for us to believe that people could have thought such strange things as this about a plant, but they did. They believed it the same way we now believe that the world is round.

There are many old books about the fields and forest, and the ones I like best are the ones that are the worst. In the old days, some of the naturalists put forth some strong arguments against the things we take as fact today. They argued that the world was flat and could not be round and turn around; if it did, the mill ponds would pour out.

There is another statement they made, though, that I find no fault with even though it is not in the books today. They said that the forest was upside down, that trees stood on their heads and stuck their tail into the air. Surely the roots are the mouth and the trunk is the body. As my mouth and body are in the reverse order, either the men or the tree is upside down.

Alabama's Room at Top, With No One in It

Alabama has always been a favorite hunting ground for world renowned botanists. This site has been visited by many of the great names in natural history. The records they kept of the things they saw in Alabama are common knowledge to naturalists today. It is not unusual to go to other states and hear people talking of the forest of our state. What really gets to you is that these people from other states know more about Alabama than Alabamians do.

Not long ago I was walking in the Talladega National Forest and met a man and his wife. They were Dr. Aldo Bracco and his wife, Maria, from Buenos Aires, Argentina. He and his wife wanted to see and learn of the plants and animals of our state before their return to South America.

Dr. Bracco is a pioneer in conservation in his country and an excellent naturalist. After several trips with them to the Bankhead, I ask Aldo how he got interested in nature. He told me that some years back he was invited on a river cruise from Buenos Aires, and on that cruise were some bird watchers from the U.S. They were looking through binoculars at the trees along the river and he asked them what they were looking at. They showed him the birds and began telling him what they were. He was embarrassed that they came to his country and knew of these things he had never seen having lived there all his life.

Today his words came back as I walked through the garden and looked at a small shrub my wife had planted there. It was the Alabama Croton, reputed to be the rarest shrub in the United States. This shrub only grows in Alabama, a short drive from Jasper. I doubt that there are more than six people in Walker County that have ever heard of it, and if they have, they likely did in some other state.

Knowledge of such things comes from exposure, it is like Bracco's birds, and having never been around anyone that knew them he never noticed them. The same is true for the people around here and the Alabama Croton.

The people that know this shrub are an elite group of worldwide botanists that have devoted their lives to a search for the rare species unknown to science. Because Alabama has never produced a botanist of any great acclaim, the state has remained a frontier for discovery. This is what brought the seekers in; it was the best place to look. The number of new or rare species a botanist finds is how many times his name is in the books. That is what determines his stature in the field.

The Alabama Croton was discovered by Dr. E.A. Smith while he was at the University. The shrub was found at Pratt's Ferry southeast of Tuscaloosa in 1877. Another location was discovered on the Warrior River between Jasper and Tuscaloosa by Dr. Mohr in 1882. These are the only two places the species has ever been seen.

By 1887 the discovery of the Alabama Croton had traveled around the world. Its description, complete with drawings, was published twice in two different publications in Germany in 1887. Yet the people that lived near them still refer to them as the "privet brakes on the river."

I guess that for a while some people around the University showed some interest in the croton, but today very few know it. The people of Alabama do not know THEIR ALABAMA CROTON because of a gross failure by the educational and governmental agencies to inform them of it.

The sites of the crotons on the Warrior River are in strip mining country and the one at Pratt's Ferry is already destroyed by bridge construction. Anytime a species is destroyed, it is not progress, it is moving backwards.

I find it strange that here close to us, both the Alabama Streak Sourus Fern, the rarest fern in the US, and the Alabama Croton, the rarest shrub in the US, at Double Springs and Tuscaloosa respectfully fell in front of the bulldozers. Bulldozers owned by the STATE OF ALABAMA and not those of a strip-miner. Alabama sure has a lot of room at the top, unfortunately there is no one in it.

Queen Anne's Lace Holds the World Together

In recent years, arts and crafts shows have become very popular in the South. Water color paintings are present at all of them and all deal with the same subject matter. The old train station, the barns, houses, and farm equipment are painted in the same setting, the weed patch; invariably the weed is always the Queen Anne's lace. That is as it should be, for this weed from Europe now covers the waste places of the US and Canada.

One reason you see it so much is because it is easy to paint.

The detail of this weed has a washed out appearance that can be "faked off." No one ever looks at a Queen Anne's lace so they don't really know what one looks like. The leaves of the plant are like those of carrot and would be very hard to paint if one was trying for realism. The only part of the plant that the mind recalls though is the cluster of flat white flowers on long green stems. The weed has the last laugh on all of us, artist and insect, for that white thing is not the flower. These heads on the stems are nearly square in the cluster and if you look closely at one you will see a tiny reddish brown dot right in the center of the white cluster. That dot is the flower.

Queen Anne's lace is a wild carrot related to the garden variety. When the flower heads start to dry up they curl up forming a bird's nest. You rarely see them used in dried flower arrangements but do see them often pressed flat. These are used in picture frames as background for mounted butterflies and moths. You find these at the arts and crafts shows also.

The Queen Anne's lace has been used by the artist but never as a medicine or a vegetable. So what can be said for the plant?

As a plant and having roots it must help hold the world together. But, since it is a carrot and has a root like one, I suspect that it does not even do a very good job of that.

Alabama's Purple Coneflowers Fading Fast

Those hot summer days that send the old folks looking for a shade and the young ones looking for a swimming hole are here again. But some things like it hot and the hotter it gets the better they like it. When the sun starts to melt the asphalt, the summer wild flowers that line the roadside are tickled pink, yellow, white, and sometimes purple.

When you speak of wildflowers, most people think of the ones that grow along the roadways. The one that their mind's eye sees is the Black Eyed Susan. Everybody knows this flower that the Cherokees call Deer's Eyes. This is one of the sunflowers or coneflowers that once covered the American prairies and meadows feeding the deer and buffalo. Those days are gone now and the coneflowers survive best between the fence and the edge of the pavement where the cow can't reach them.

Most all the coneflowers are yellow with black or brown centers. There is one that is purple. Its Latin name is *Echinacea purpurea*—that, in plain English, is "purple hedgehog." It gets this name from the center of the flower that looks like a hedgehog with his quills up.

A few years ago, a friend called from Moulton and told my wife that she knew where a patch of purple coneflowers were and that a housing project was going to be built on the site. She went to the site near Moulton and brought a clump back. They have done well and bloomed every year since.

In all my wanderings, I do not recall ever seeing a purple coneflower. They are a large, pale purple wild flower and grow in open places where they are easy to see. If they were plentiful I would surely have seen one. Because no one else seems to have seen any either, I always assumed them very rare and not native to this part of the country.

When you are not very smart you have to have books to prop yourself up with and if you are not very smart at all you need many books. In my case, I have books on the plants of Alabama that began in 1775 and continue up until today. The one I like best was printed in 1889 and has everything listed in alphabetical order. While using this book to check the spelling of the Latin name, I also found out that this flower was common from the Gulf Coast to Pennsylvania and Iowa. This did not seem possible. I started checking its range then in later publications and as the books progressed with the years the range would get smaller each time.

The most recent books tell a story that is even worse concerning the future of the purple coneflower. The Wildflower book of North Carolina does not list or picture this flower. The Kentucky Wildflower and the Alabama Wildflower books say it is rare and infrequently seen in these states. If that was not enough to make you wonder about its future, the US Forest Service has even listed it as a rare and threatened species.

One thing is for sure, the purple coneflower that was common in the eastern US one hundred years ago is fading fast in Alabama.

Opossum: Grinning Critter Well Known Here

Of all the animals around us, none is better known than the opossum. This animal has many strange words used to describe it. The one I like best is 'sikwautsets,' which is the Indian name that translates as "smiling pig." The way the opossum's mouth is shaped makes him look as if he was smiling. You hear of this quite often as people refer to one another as *"grinning like a possum."*

You see drawings of the opossum hanging by his tail. He can do it, but never does in the wild. He has what is called a prehensile tail which is one that can be used like a finger. He uses it to climb with, but not to hang by. This critter's mouth is as odd as his tail. He has 50 teeth, more than any other mammal in the United States. It is said that if he bites you he will not

let go until it thunders. I doubt if that is true, for if it was, there would be a lot of people walking around with opossums hanging on them.

Another strange word used to describe his eating habit is omnivorous. That means he will eat anything. That I believe. Yet I always seem to associate them with the persimmon trees, knowing they prefer roadside garbage. I would be more logical to associate one with a car, for it is from a car they are most often seen.

You would think that after a while the opossums would all be killed as many as you see dead on the road. Not a chance, the ratty looking creatures have from five to twenty in a litter. When they are born they are the size of a pinto bean. The mother carries them in a pouch until they get too big; then they all climb out and ride on her back. Only about a half dozen of a litter survive, but that is more than enough.

The opossum is the only marsupial on the North American continent. Nearly all of the mammals that carry their young in a pouch for some reason live south of the equator. None of these marsupials were known to exist before the discovery of America, and I wonder what the Europeans thought when the explorers went home and told of the large rats that carried their babies in a pocket and hung in the trees by their tails.

We do know what happened when the first explorer went home from Australia and told of what he saw. A large animal that had the head of a deer, the front legs of a squirrel, the hind legs of a rabbit, and carried its baby in a pouch on its stomach and stood on its tail. They thought he was crazy. Yet his description of a kangaroo is very accurate.

It is sometimes hard to describe things that have never been seen before. But this was never a problem for primitive man as much as it is with us. Unlike ourselves, they searched for the new and different. They used few words and made better use of them. The Indian name for the automobile was "di-tulena," which means "it stares." That describes the car as well as their word describes the opossum.

The opossum plays an important part in the nature of the Southern forest. It is a primary food source for all the larger meat eaters—foxes, bobcats, coyotes, hawks and owls. The woods would not be the same without him. He is a slow moving creature and easy to catch and provides a large meal.

For a number of years, I tracked mountain lions in North Alabama. In all those years, I found only two kills that were conclusively mountain lion. One was a deer and the other was an opossum.

Have You Ever Met the Saddle Back Moth?

The old timers had a way of remembering things by the way they were marked. These signs, while great for identifying things, often went beyond all logic. Naturalists use the same marks or signs for the same reason. There is no better means for quickly identifying species in the field.

Our two poisonous spiders, the Black Widow and the Brown Recluse, respectively are marked with a red hourglass and a brown violin. Neither of these signs have anything to do with poison. Had Mother Nature intended these signs as such, she would have marked them with skulls and crossbones. Mother Nature never heard of a violin or hourglass, these are manmade things. To be realistic, we have to occasionally remember who and where we are.

The three general divisions of living things are plants, animals and insects. There are 250,000 kinds of plants, 215,000 kinds of animals, and a whopping 625,000 species of insects. Some experts think there may be even a million kinds of insects if they were all identified. This is the age of the insect. It is the most typical form of life on earth. Yet we know very little about them. The only ones we remember are the ones that give us reason.

We see the little brown moth flapping around the light and think nothing of it. However, when that same moth was crawling around with a brown saddle on his back, we knew him well.

This critter the old timers sometimes called a packsaddle is really the Saddle Back Moth. The hairy looking spines on this caterpillar are connected to glands that produce poison. When he crawls on you or you brush against him, you know it for sure.

You don't hear as much about Saddle Backs as you used to due to modern machinery. Mechanical corn, cotton, and pea pickers have raised the farmers up above them. This does not mean they are not here; there are probably more now than ever, we are just not exposed to them.

All hairy caterpillars are not poisonous. The tent caterpillar that builds those nests in cherry trees has spines that are indigestible. The Rain Crow is the only bird that will eat them. They would kill any other bird.

When the spines become imbedded in the stomach lining of the Rain Crow, he sheds his stomach lining and grows a new one. He is the only one that can do that.

There is something else that eats tent caterpillars, and that's bream. They make great fish bait.

Please Keep Off the Leaves, If You Will

Did you ever stand with a rake in your hand and wonder why some trees were evergreen and others not? Well, it's all in the leaves. Some trees have leaves that mature in one year and are bare in the winter.

The others have leaves that mature in two years, thus the evergreens have two crops of leaves on them at the same time. After the second year they shed one crop yearly.

Some plants have leaves that only grow in the winter. Hepatica, known for its medical properties, puts on new leaves in the spring before the trees leaf out. When the trees shade the forest floor the leaves of this plant stop growing.

After the leaves fall and the light reaches the ground again, the leaves of the Hepatica start growing again, and grow all winter. This plant is adapted to live in a hardwood forest. You will never see a Hepatica under a pine or any other evergreen.

The portion that falls from a tree in one piece determines what is called the leaf. A hickory has several leaflets on one stem, the leaf is the stem and all the leaflets combined. The cowcumber is often thought of as having the largest leaf. However, the devil's walking stick has the largest because of the mass of leaflets it has on a single stem.

The oddest leaf around here grows on the beadly oaks in Kaiser Bottoms. This tree has only recently been identified and is not yet in the books. This area has a large variety of oaks, including the cow oaks and overcups not often seen.

Some trees have more than one kind of leaf. The sassafras has three different shapes. One is entire, one mitten shaped, and one twice cleft.

The basswood has a leaf with a flower growing out of it. As for the habits and shapes of leaves, the peculiarities have no end. The saddest thing about leaves is a true story. Many early explorers that came to this country suffered from dysentery. This is caused from a vitamin deficiency. The leaves of the hemlock tree are rich in this vitamin. A tea made from the leaves will both prevent and cure dysentery. Yet many of the explorers suffered and died under hemlock trees.

Many of the insects bear the names of the leaves they prefer to feed on, like the hackberry butterfly, the tulip tree moth, and the cherry moth. Sometimes, however, the insects or the people who name them get things mixed up.

The laurel sphinx eats grand-sire-greybeards, walnut moths eat hickory, and the hawk moth eats sweet potato vines. Leaves are in a league all their own. Most everything in the forest is directly dependent on them for survival. A favorite trick of natural history teachers is to mark off one square foot in the leaves and have the students sift through them listing what they find. The amount of life forms found in that space is awesome.

In some cases the naturalist tends to be over protective.

After years of studying life in a leaf mold, they know what is there even before they look. They know each critter personally, the way most people know their friends. It is for that reason that they sometimes get upset when you walk on the leaves.

I can appreciate that not because of biology, but because of the old mountain man who introduced me to the forest. He sat me down in the woods and said, "You must learn to see with your ears. If you look with your eyes you will never see anything. You can never set foot in the woods that not a million eyes are looking at you."

Then he started showing them to me. He had no fancy names for them, but he knew them all.

Backwoodsmen Barking Up Wrong Bush

Sipsey Wilderness has an endless list of outstanding wild flowers native to the State of Alabama. Of those, the wild hydrangea best represents the state as a whole. It is found in all of Alabama except the southwestern extremes near the coast. It would have been our best state flower, had not our lawmakers names a Japanese potted plant to represent the state.

The Oak Leaved Hydrangea is well known to all and is called Seven Bark in Alabama. It was found in Alabama and named in Alabama by William Bartram. Its large white blooms turn wine in the Fall and brown in the Winter. With blooms that remain year-round, the Seven Bark is more abundant in our state than it is anywhere else in its range. No state has a native state flower with the qualifications than the Seven Bark had to offer this one.

The Seven Bark is almost indestructible. The more the

plant is abused, the better it spreads. The more the flowers are picked, the more it blooms. Yet we in Alabama passed over this shrub for a Japanese Camellia.

SEVEN BARK

Our state has another wild hydrangea that is not as well known as the Seven Bark because its flowers are not as showy. It is called Nine Bark in Alabama. This one has round leaves rather than those shaped like an oak. The wild hydrangeas are a perfect example of why plants have Latin names. The Seven Bark (*Hydrangea querifolia*) and the Nine Bark (*Hydrangea aboresecens*) have their common names or numbers reversed in different parts of their ranges. The best common names are the Oak Leaved and the Smooth Hydrangeas. The numerical names are rarely found in printed matter.

What the woodsmen call Seven Bark in the Smokies and what they call Seven Bark in Alabama are two different plants. So, what's the big deal?

One of the wild hydrangeas is an official medical plant. The Smooth Hydrangea called Nine Bark in Alabama is called Seven Bark in Tennessee. A drug made from this plant is said to be effective in preventing kidney stones. Confused? Wait till you take your medicine and the herb digger has … BARKED UP THE WRONG BUSH.

Rare Turtle Found in Sipsey

How often do we cross the bridges here in the Warrior Basin and never notice a thing. In our ramblings through the country we never give any thought to the world of wild things, except maybe a brief one when the cottontail crosses the road.

Yet we live and work in one of the most unique communities of plants and animals in North America. As children we have heard many tales of the creatures around us, most often not based in truth. Some of us know little about the game species but these are so few they furnish no knowledge of the rare and unusual.

One such creature is the flattened musk turtle. This rare turtle lives only in the Warrior River north of Tuscaloosa, most of them in the Sipsey Fork.

This little turtle is no larger than a man's hand and varies in color from a moss green to a muddy brown. It is easily recognized by its flat shell.

This turtle is known to biologists as the *Sternotherus minor depressus.* The watercolor illustration was painted from a live turtle that was caught and then released on Clear Creek 14 miles north of Jasper. The future of this species is uncertain. It is considered a threatened species by the Alabama Museum of Natural History and the Southwestern Wildlife Society but has not yet made the federal endangered list.

Its entire range is in the coal-mining district Warrior Basin. It has a need for clean, un-impounded water and its sur-

Sterothaerus depressus.

Manasca

FLATTENED MUSK TURTLE

vival is in question.

And, like everyone else, I ask myself, what is this turtle worth? Not much, I guess.

But neither was the ivory-billed woodpecker, the wolf, the cougar, the eagle, or the eastern wood buffalo that once roamed Alabama.

Consider that right now there are 106 rare and endangered plant species in Alabama and 65 shell fish that are endangered, 15 of which are possibly already extinct.

Eight of the 26 endangered fish in Alabama may already be extinct. Fifteen reptiles and amphibians along with 11 species of birds and seven animals in Alabama are fighting for their lives.

Maybe they have some right to be here too. That may not be a very popular thought around here, so we just don't say anything.

Wanted: one set of mule blinders.

Literary Pursuit of the Dreaded Joint Snake

Seeing as how both Christian and heathen are equally afeared of snakes, men must have an in-born fear of them; a fear that has led to an almost endless variety of tales about them. Some of us remember the old days when the yard around the house was as wild as the woods are now. There were more snakes then or maybe it just seemed so because we were closer to them.

The deadly puff adders were seen quite often, setting panic in the people. Me, too, because I have been told of the danger they posed.

The puff adder, however, is the most harmless snake in the country. This non-poisonous snake does not even open his mouth when he strikes at a person. He is all bluff, bumping with his nose. It works quite well, thought, and scares the devil out of you.

But the fact remains that for a person to be bitten by one, he would have to put his finger in the snake's mouth and step on its head. The puff adder is actually the hognose snake which eats nothing but toads.

The most widespread and outrageous tales are without doubt those of the "joint snake."

To kill a joint snake you first scream like a dying panther. You then get the hoe handle humming like the blades on a helicopter, cutting the snake into as many pieces as possible. Once the dust settles, you scatter the pieces to the four winds or once it is dark they will crawl back together again.

The truth is that the joint snake is not even a snake. It is a legless lizard and has two things no snake has—eyelids and ears. This snake-looking lizard is almost two-thirds tail. Like any lizard, its tail will break off. When the lizard is hit with a flat object the tail will break into many pieces. These tail pieces will wiggle violently, holding your attention while the business end crawls away; where it will survive to grow a new one.

The smooth appearance and the fragileness of the joint snake gives it its true name, the glass lizard.

Once the glass lizard starts to regenerate a new tail the new growth will be smaller and a different color. This makes the lizard appear to have a spike on the end of his tail.

Presto… you now have a horn snake. It has a stinger on its tail that can strike and kill a white oak tree.

The horn snake, however, is not a snake. It is a legless lizard. It has two things that snakes don't have – eyelids and ear holes.

Driving up Alabama 195 the other day, I saw a glass lizard cross the road and for a brief moment I was back in my childhood. I could see the old homes setting high on rock pillars with their yard scraped and swept clean.

I could see the brush broom and the old hoe blade with a hole in it for the handle to be driven through. The yard so clean that nothing could pass unseen: Chickens chased the bugs and the people chased the snakes.

It is said that the closer man lives to nature the more supernatural are his beliefs and that as he moves away from raw nature the more natural his beliefs become. Some people, though, just don't seem to believe in anything and spend a lot of time trying to convince us they believe in everything.

The glass lizard has been found near the Black Pond Community, and its picture was taken by Mike Hopiak. He has since become the supervisor of wildlife photography at Cornell University in New York.

The good ones always get away.

Barred Owl: Laughing Bird of Prey Provides Chills

The noisiest creature in the forest has to be the barred owl. He is the owl everyone knows as the hoot owl and his WHO-WHO are YOU have chilled the spine of many kids on their first camping trip. He can make a variety of sounds that few would think came from a bird.

He has an attraction to light that will often bring him on silent wings to a tree near the camp fire. His favorite trick is to sit quietly for hours and then suddenly cut loose with a scream like a bobcat. This unexpected noise has sent many a camper clamoring through the pots and pans.

He has a series of HEES, HOOS and HAWS he puts together in groups of threes that sound like hysterical laughter. This strange sound of an Alabama bird is sometimes heard in the background of Tarzan movies. The first time I heard one do this, I was a kid in the forest with one of my mountain peers. Shocked by the sound, I asked him what it was. He replied with a grin, "he did not know,

Barred Owl

183

but it sounded like it just set down on a feather." I later learned that his old mountain joke was older than he was.

In the spring mating season, the barred owls will get together in groups of as many as a half dozen and all start laughing at the same time. When this happens, the whole forest will rattle. Once you have stayed around these owls for a while you can tell one from the other as easy as you can tell one farm rooster from another. It is not uncommon for a barred owl to live 20 years, so you have plenty of time to learn them as individuals.

The old barred owl is the one people see the most. He is not above hunting in the daytime and is quite active about an hour before dark. They love water and bathe often. They seem to always be hanging around creeks and branches in most all types of forest.

He is the owl that turkey hunters call the laughing owl. In the spring, the turkey will gobble when he hears his hoot. The mark of a turkey hunter is how well he can hoot to a turkey in order to locate him before he starts his turkey calling.

One thing about him, he is not squeamish about what he eats. He will eat anything from a frog to a Mayfly, a green bean to a rattlesnake. The only thing he won't eat is a shrew but neither will anything else. His favorite food seems to be small snakes, which he eats with little fanfare.

Pouncing on the snake with his feet, the owl will pen him and bite it just behind the head breaking the spine. He then swallows the snake head first an inch at a time while it is still wiggling. He will then sit with his eyes half closed while the snake wiggles inside him making the breast feathers go up and down.

No matter who told you an owl could turn his head all the way around; it is not true. A barred owl can only turn his head half way around. The great horned owl can get his three-quarters around before he has to unwind. They do have an incredible ability to see small objects at great distances and a hearing ability far superior to man.

Barred owls are protected in Alabama as are all birds of prey. Only in recent years has man learned that the owls were performing a beneficial service and deserved a better deal. The woods would not be the same without them.

Beavers Play Active Role in Demise of Chinquapin

Not long ago, every fourth tree in the hardwood forest was a chestnut. Then the blight came, killing every one of them east of the Mississippi. The disease, carried on the feet of woodpeckers, traveled at a rate of 24 miles a year. One woodpecker was found to be carrying 5,000 spores on its feet. The chestnut never had a chance.

We tend to think that the chestnut blight only lived on that tree alone. The truth is that it also lives on hickory, oak, maple, sumac, and chinquapin. The chinquapin is as susceptible to the disease as the chestnut. This small tree grows faster and seeds faster than the chestnut, so the destruction is not as noticeable as it was on the chestnut. You don't hear as much about it as you did when the chestnut was dying because the chinquapin has no commercial value. The only thing considered in the Southern forest anymore seems to be the dollar.

In the past 10 years, some of the largest stands of chinquapins have vanished completely. One I have been watching was lost to reforestation. The trees were injured when the area was logged and replanted with heavy equipment. This disease enters the trees through injured places. Now, not a single sprout remains where this thicket once stood.

This is happening throughout the whole forest. Chinquapins are becoming scarce and in a very short time will disappear from the forest completely. No steps are being taken to preserve this species. There are several different kinds of chinquapins in the state, but the rarest of them all is the Alabama Chinquapin. This one only grows in Alabama and has always been an uncommon species. Today it is rare, and endangered. It won't do any good to look this one up on the federal list, the EPA never heard of it and Alabama has no "endangered species" according to our state government.

The Alabama Chinquapin is easy to tell from all the others. It has large leaves like a chestnut but has rough bark that keeps it from looking like a chestnut sprout. It only grows on sandy creek banks in Alabama. Browns Creek on the Rocky Plains has the best habitat in the state, yet they are very rare there. When the beavers were reintroduced in the area they flooded the habitat drowning the trees. The only place they can survive now is on the side streams above the beaver line.

It is a different story with the possumhaw. Before it could only live in the cutoffs or oxbows along the original creeks. Now it can travel all over the bottoms never getting its feet out of the water. This is a story of nature and changing times causing hardship for one and good times for another, a story that equally applies to man.

It was not long ago that everyone knew the chinquapin. Now few would even recognize it. They know the name but not the tree. They no longer have reason to. With advances in farming and marketing, people no longer survive by knowledge of the earth; they just survive. They grow further and further away from nature.

ALABAMA CHINQUAPIN

This drawing away is what causes environmental problems. These problems are caused by ignorance and not progress. The big loss will be to the individual through his loss of that very important sense of belonging; the sense that can only be found through knowledge of who he is and where he is.

I, like everyone else, was taught that it was all right to take anything I wanted from the forest or do anything I wanted to the water or air or whatever as long as it was in the name of progress. I was taught a lie and now we are all beginning to feel the consequences.

So now we look to the sky searching for other "inhabitable planets," convincing ourself that it would be easier to find one out there somewhere than to take care of the one we have.

I wander off to the swamp to get away from it all, down to Kaeiser Spring where the chinquapin grows. While I viewed the chinquapin and possumhaw growing side by side, in the back of my mind I saw John Burroughs with his long white beard and his baggy black suit and heard again those words he wrote 80 years ago…

It is well to stop our star-gazing occasionally and consider the ground under our feet. Maybe it is celestial, too; maybe this brown, sun-tanned, sin-stained earth is a sister to the morning and evening star. If it should turn out to be so, it seems to me we have many things to learn over again—we must tear down and build larger.

No wonder the old fathers resisted the notion that the earth was round and turned round! It was not the mill-ponds that were in danger of spilling out as much as certain creeds and theories.

Legend is Gone, but Name Remains

Once you begin learning the names of plants, you realize that an unusually large number of them are called snakeroots… a number so large they could never have been used to treat snake bites.

Not in history has that many people been bitten.

There is a plant that grows here called Sampson's snakeroot. It is one of the gentians (GEN shun). This family of wildflowers has blooms that rarely open. This gives one of them its common name of closed, or bottle, gentian.

Of the several species of gentians native to Alabama, Sampson's snakeroot is the only one with straw colored flowers. This makes it easy to identify. Gentians as a whole are not very common. In Alabama, three of the gentians are considered endangered species. The Sampson's is one of them.

Many of the old legends about plants were supernatural rather than medical. Most were carried and a few taken. A Sampson's snakeroot carried was supposed to increase ones strength.

Many plants were carried to ward off snakes. Those were marked with a sign of some sort. Downy rattlesnake plantain was one because the veins in the leaves look like a snake's skin. This marking was called the "doctrine of signatures."

The name would imply that Sampson's snakeroot got its name from white settlers. The Indians were big on signatures but were not afraid of snakes.

Whatever the case; carrying a Sampson's snakeroot was to make one stronger and safe from snakes. The legend is gone but the name remains.

Rare Club Moss is Found in Sipsey

Ground Cedar, Alabama's little known and seldom seen club moss, is said to have been common in North Alabama at one time. Old records state that the sale of Ground Cedar as Christmas green was "a prominent business" in Chattanooga, being collected in "great amounts" in North Alabama. This may be why it is so extremely rare here today. It is so rare, in fact, that many of the botanists in Alabama have never seen it in the wild. Many of them have spent a lifetime in the woods looking for it while searching for other plants. All of them know the plant but, like myself, learned it out of state.

It is the type of thing that if you ever see it you never forget it. It grows on a trailing vine and sends up little stems about six inches tall that look like cedar trees. These form mats that cover the ground.

This club moss, considered a plant of the northern mountains, has been recorded only three times in our state in the last 60 years. In 1920, a colony was found on Miller's Creek in Jackson County. In 1962, it was seen on Cheaha Mountain in Clay County, and in 1969 in the Bankhead Forest in Lawrence

County. These locations are very small and a large site is in Lawrence County.

A few odd sprigs have been seen in Jackson County, and I have heard that a little may be growing at Camp McDowell. Recent finds indicate that this plant may have grown further south than anyone suspected.

A few weeks ago, on a small creek 10 miles north of Jasper, a colony of this rare club moss was discovered that may be the largest single site in existence. This site covers over 1000 square feet in one solid mat.

The size of this colony alone is sufficient to verify that is growing naturally. It has been there for a long, long time. This places Walker County at the top of the list and no one ever suspected it grew here. It will be interesting to see how long it will survive.

Camellia: The State Flower Carries "Made In" Label

Most people are surprised to learn that Alabama has two species of camellias native to this state. Wild Camellias are found in all counties but are most abundant in Walker and Winston counties.

In all other southern states, only two counties can boast of having both species. On the planet earth, Poplar Springs in southern Winston County is the only place they grow side by side.

The camellia greatly resembles the dogwood tree, only having a flatter top. The large blooms lie flat against the leaves, producing a situation where you can walk under a million and never see one. They bloom after the dogwoods have gone.

So next time you see a late blooming dogwood, look again; it may be a camellia.

The Silky Camellia has a white bloom with a deep purple center. The Mountain Camellia has a center that varies from purple or orange to a pale yellow. The Mountain Camellia is the most numerous in Walker and Winston, with orange centers.

The largest single stand of camellias I know of is in the Dogtown Community of Carbon Hill. If you look for camellias in this area of the state, do it in May and June.

Walk the hillsides looking down on the tops of the small trees that line the banks of the creeks. You are sure to see one. The Silky Camellia is also found on the shore of Smith Lake in the Bankhead National Forest.

Alabama is the camellia state, but it is not a native species.

The state flower is the bloom from what was once a tree native to China and Japan developed through mutations into the Camellia Japonica. Alabama's state flower is in every sense of the phrase and in all truth, "Made in Japan."

No one was happy with the native Goldenrod as state flower but with the native flora we should have been. A small group of camellia growers convinced the state legislature to name the Japonica our state flower. Even a native weed is better than this.

Mississippi has its magnolia, Georgia has its Cherokee Rose, and Alabama has its JAPANESE POTTED PLANT.

Never, Ever Take a Shrew to Dinner, Pal

The most unusual animal we have here in the Warrior Basin is no doubt the long-nose shrew.

The smallest animal alive is the Pygmy Shrew. He weighs from one-ninth to one-seventh of an ounce. This places our long-nose shrew a very close second with a full grown adult weighing about the same as a dime.

The long-nose shrew has been placed on the state's rare

animal list as a species of special concern. It will most likely become an endangered species when more research is done on him.

Only about 700 long-nose shrews have ever been recorded and 300 of those were from Alabama. When you compare him to the snail darters that number in the thousands, you realize just how rare he is.

We have two colonies near Jasper; one is at the Clear Creek Resort and the other is near the previous Arrow Trailer Park in east Jasper.

This little brown shrew has a life span of about one year. His scientific name is *Sorex longirostris* which means "long nosed."

This is also our only poisonous mammal. Nature has equipped the shrew with poisonous saliva to help him kill his prey. He has a nasty disposition and bites when handled. His bite can cause pain and discomfort to humans.

Shrews are noted for many things. They have been described for nearly 2000 years. Ancient people believed that having some around the house would ward off evil spirits.

These little creatures have hearts that beat 1,200 times per minute. That demands a great deal of food. This causes a shrew to eat twice his own weight daily.

Man-size, he would have to eat 300 pounds of food a day. Never take a shrew to lunch.

World's Rarest Buckeye Abounds in Sipsey

Some folks tell me that buckeyes are poison; others tell me buckeyes bring luck. The list of things they will cure is endless. I carried one for a while and the pains in my joints worsened,

Roland M. Harper

and my luck ran out. The only good part was that I did not die, so they must be safe enough.

There are so many different species of buckeyes; it is possibly I was carrying the wrong kind. The rarest buckeye is the white buckeye, which is commonly found in Sipsey Country.

This shrub is so little known that most of the best reference books don't even list it. The only authority on this plant was the late Dr. Roland Harper of the University of Alabama. He said, "*There is more white buckeye in Alabama than in all the rest of the world combined. After looking for this plant for years, I am convinced that this is so.*"

Roland McMillan Harper was born in Farmington, Maine, on August 11, 1878, and served as a botanist for the Geological Survey of Alabama until his death. He was one of the last botanists to describe native vegetation in the Southeast before it was altered by human activity; his diaries, journals, publications, and photographs are in the W. S. Hoole Special Collections Library at the University

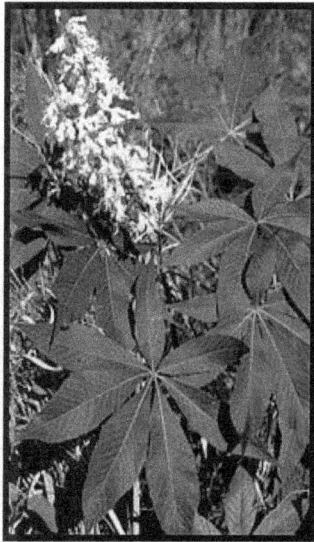
White Buckeye

of Alabama. Harper died on April 30, 1966, and is buried in Tuscaloosa Memorial Park.

No area in the state has had its plants recorded to the extent that the Sipsey Region has, yet the photograph shown here might be the only white buckeye in the whole county. Moving just south of Jasper you start to see them everywhere.

This buckeye is ornamental and has a way of popping up unexpectedly in botanical gardens. It was named by William Bartram and was most likely better known in his time than it is now. Most people call it the bottlebrush bush.

Dr. Hall of Florence tells me that a few years ago while in England, he was asked if he might look at a plant they could not identify. He was shocked to see a white buckeye.

Ivory Bill: No Place to Go But Away

The Ivory-Billed Woodpecker, while listed as an engendered species in Alabama, is most likely extinct in this state. It was last recorded in our state in 1907, but was in 1950 near the Florida state line, so chances are slim that it is still with us.

There is no way now to save the species. This bird lives in

dying virgin timber and that timber is gone. Days are numbered for any still alive.

People often think they have seen one when they see

a Woodhen. Woodhens are big, but the Ivory Bill was even bigger. They are different in appearance in that the ivory bill has more white on his wings and, of course, an ivory bill. The Woodhen has a black bill.

At one time, ivory bills must have been numerous in the state because of the numbers of bills found in Indian diggings. They seem to have preferred the south part of the state but have been seen around the Millport area west of Fayette in 1886. It is doubtful that any good picture of this bird was ever taken due to his existence in a time prior to telephoto lens.

Bald Eagles are seen regularly on Smith Lake, and the red-cockaded woodpecker at times is found around here in numbers. The little Bachman warbler, though not lately seen, may still be here. But of all these endangered species of birds native to Alabama, the possibility of seeing an Ivory Bill is almost zero.

Though all these birds are now protected by federal law, it will do America's largest, most beautiful woodpecker no good.

Lesson of Trailing Arbutus

Living in the house dulls one's senses. We have grown so accustomed to controlled temperatures in the home, office, and car that the changing seasons have little effect. It makes one, to a degree, lose touch with reality.

When you live with nature as the Indians did, the changing of the seasons is most evident. As the days grow colder and the sun moves to the south, you know it will stop and start its journey north soon. When it reaches the place of the winter sunrise, life's cycle for the year has ended.

The winter sunrise is the most celebrated day in history.

All the old people took this day to honor the creator God. The ancients in Germany on this occasion paid respect to the God of New Life and called it the yule season.

At this time of the year, a living tree was brought into the house as a God symbol and gifts to the creator were tied to the branches. The homes were decorated with holly and ivy on this the grandest of all German holidays.

When Christianity came to Germany, a day was needed to celebrate the birth of Christ. They chose this same day as it was already a national holiday. The date made no difference as the day of Christ's birth is unknown.

Soon the tree became a symbol of Christmas.

When Christmas came to America, the tree and the cutting of the ivy came with it. The decorating with a wreath made it necessary to use native vines. Electricity and tinfoil were unheard of.

In America, two native vines were used: trailing arbutus and bamboo vine. As the eastern cities grew, the woods were pushed further and further away. In time, the trees and vines were shipped into town.

From Alabama came the bamboo vine. This is an Alabama saw briar, an evergreen. It has more leaves than the one we see so much of. It grows mostly along creeks around here. There was one place in Alabama from which so much bamboo vine was shipped that the town was named for it: Evergreen, Alabama.

Trailing arbutus is a more northerly species but does grow here also. It was shipped by the train-car loads in the north. It was ripped up to the extent that in some states, it was almost destroyed. This prompted these states to pass laws to protect it, which did little good.

When a species gets in trouble, you protect it, and it will

recover on its own. This did not work for the trailing arbutus.

It cannot be grown from seeds, transplanted, grown from cutting, or increased by any efforts of man. It cannot withstand heavy logging operations and has little resistance to fire.

The only place that it will survive will be in eastern wilderness areas.

The trailing arbutus was growing near Pinetuckey Church a few years ago and is now dead. It died in a logging operation on public owned land, in a national forest timber sale. Since 1950, the US Forest Service has killed the arbutus accidentally on more than 50,000 acres of the Bankhead alone.

INDIAN HERITAGE OF SIPSEY

The vine covered rock piles and dug wells are all that now mark the old log cabin home sites in the wilderness. Several of those old cabins were around the Wolf Pen Area. Wolf Pen was the name of a log church that was also a school and had a small cemetery nearby. All signs of these historic sites are now gone except for the cemetery. The massive red oaks that once shaded the site were girdled and killed by the U.S. Forest Service. The site was then cut through twice by road improvements.

Wolf Pen is now gone but the memory lives on in the hearts and minds of those who knew it. Mrs. Louvina Athel Gertrude Tidwell Watts remembers the place well; she went to school there. Her parents lived on the boundary of what is now the Sipsey Wilderness Area. She remembers as a child how she and her brother roamed the forest digging star root. She tells me that the star root patches were larger than they are now. *"The woods burned then and the seeds could reach the ground,"* she said. I too have noticed this.

She said, *"I do not remember the forest as being wild; neither did my dad, but when you know a place or love it, it never is wild no matter how wild it really is."* She speaks of how they raised their own food and only bought coffee, flour, sugar, and salt. Her father would cut cross ties and square them with an ax for 25 cents each, in times when five dollars' worth of coffee cost 10 cents.

As of 1981, Mrs. LouvinaWatts lived in the Thach Community with her mother, Mrs. Lula Arkedelphia Margaret Ingledove Garrison Tidwell Thomas Miller Long. On the 26th of August, 1981, she celebrated her 94th birthday. Mrs. Lula

Long was reared in the forest as were her parents, the Garrisons of mixed Celtic and Indian ancestry. Alonzo and Louvina Garrison's beginnings in the forest are now a dim memory in the distant past. Mrs. Long still remembers Aunt Jenny Brooks Johnson, who was half Cherokee Indian; she was the best known product of the Sipsey Wilderness.

Mrs. Long had a brother, Andrew Garrison, who lived in Haleyville, and a sister, Evie Gray, who lived in Tennessee. From Mrs. Long's humble and peaceful beginnings in the forest has out-lived four husbands. In 1981, she had 79 living direct descendants. She said, "*The thing that brought the people into the forest was the peace and quiet and a desire for elbow room.*" This is the same thing that brings them here today, but in the early days isolation meant protection from removal for those of mixed Indian ancestry.

At the head of Parker Branch Canyon there is a waterfall. Below the falls is a cathedral cove that offers the most peaceful setting that one could ask for. On one of the beech trees is written, *BILL TIDWELL 1912...PRAYED TO GOD.* This is the perfect place for a man to come to be alone with his maker and I have often wondered who he was... As I sat and talked with Mrs. Watts and her mother, her father Bill Tidwell looked down at me from an old oval picture frame.

Bill Tidwell, born Oct. 8, 1882, died at the age of 37. While doing a good deed for a neighbor, he contracted a little germ called tuberculosis. He carried it home and died, as did six or seven of his brothers and sisters. Bill Tidwell's prayer is now in the Sipsey Wilderness and will never be cut, girted, poisoned, or sold to a hungry paper mill as so many others have been in the Bankhead National Forest. The tree will stand as long as nature's God will allow, insured by Act of Congress. The tree shall stand and be available should Bill Tidwell's great-great-grand-children need it for the same reason he did.

Those people that preserved the wilderness had just this thing in mind as they fought to preserve. They were called nature lovers and all sorts of names by the pulpwood growers, saying they were dreamers accursed with too many emotions, standing in the way of progress.

Jim Manasco said, "*Well, I cast my lot with Tidwell and the nature lovers because they deal in reality and not computerized assumptions. I'm for saving all of the Bankhead Forest for the same reason the aforementioned wanted only part and it may happen yet for there are more people talking to the trees now than ever before.*"

Indians on Rocky Plains

The Rocky Plains is the boundary corner of the Indian Nations. The Cherokee were to the northeast, Chickasaw to the northwest, the Choctaw to the southwest, and Creeks to the southeast.

The Indians seem to have used this land jointly as a hunting ground. The first white men to the area were squatters in the late 1700s, mostly married to Indians. Later some came through going to the Battle of New Orleans in 1812, but most of those who remained came into the area with Andrew Jackson in the Creek Indian uprising in 1814.

There are many graveyards on the Plains, and many of them are of unknown origins. The oldest site on the Plains that is still intact is the old Rocky Plains Church. It is secluded deep in the woods on an unmarked road. Local people keep it in excellent repair. In the cemetery, there are veterans of the war of 1812 and the Civil War buried next to each other. Some of the older graves in the more remote regions of the Plains now have huge trees growing in them.

The west side of the Plains follows Browns Creek. In 1851, a man called Doctor Andrew Kaeiser settled here. No single man in history has brought as much chaos to the Town of Jasper as this one did.

Blood Across Sipsey

During the period of the Civil War, it is hard to understand how so many hard times could befall those peace-loving people who lived in the Sipsey area. It did though, and before it ended it had reached all the way to Oklahoma. For most, the hard times were brought on the people of the Sipsey area by one man who came late and left early.

This section of Alabama had been a refuge for people who wanted most in life to just be left alone. That is what brought them here and that is about all the area was good for. It was too rough to cross and too rocky to plow, but peaceful solitude was plentiful here in a place that no one wanted.

With the Indian Removal Act of May 28, 1830, many Indians came into the area looking for a hiding place. They mixed well with the white settlers, for they were the same kind of people; most were Scots Irish Cherokee mixed-bloods. The times were changing and dark clouds were coming to the mountains of Sipsey in the form of mineral waters. The peaceful days were ending.

The new craze was mineral spring's resorts that could cure anything. They were cropping up all down the Tennessee River bringing the rich northern trade with them. People were getting wealthy selling water. None of the local people ever had a dream of getting rich in such a manner, but others did.

A little known sheriff's deputy in the Tennessee Valley by the name of Andrew Kaeiser came up the mountain. In 1851 he bought the unwanted government lands along Browns Creek for $1.25 an acre. This tract of land has more springs per square foot than most places had by the square mile. Doctor Andrew Kaeiser was bottling and selling his healing waters. He was one of the few men in Winston County who had slaves—20 of them. Anyone who had that number of slaves was exempted from fighting in the Civil War. Those who had less or none had to fight.

It was a rich man's war and a poor man's battle, so Kaeiser did his civic duty and stayed home serving as an informant for the Home Guard. The guard went into the hills of Sipsey to bring out those who would not fight. Those who did not come out to fight in the rich man's war were killed in many different ways to provide sadistic amusement for the Confederate Home Guard.

It was Dr. Kaeiser who was telling the Home Guard who they were and where they were hiding. The number of people who Kaeiser fingered for death is unbelievable, but the historic records are correct. Yet the people did not retaliate in any manner to speak of.

The freedom with which the Home Guard was allowed to go through the mountainous countryside doing as they pleased also allowed them to take from the Southern sympathizers likewise. Soon even these were complaining about their own Home Guard. The weapons that they used were provided by the state. The Reverend James H. Hill of Jasper, Kaesier's alter-ego, was the man who supplied and stored them.

Hill's Jasper-based operations in 1864 were holding several unionist prisoners for execution, but the Tories had enough.

After Hill realized this, he disbanded his guard and fled for his life, never to return. On the morning of the execution, 26 men met on the Rocky Plains of Sipsey and rode against Jasper.

Charging Jasper, they went straight way to the jail and freed the prisoners; they then made the jailer burn the jail. They also burned the courthouse, academy, and several other buildings. The group swelled in numbers by the prisoners headed back to the mountains of Sipsey.

Kaesier was killed and his house burned; his wife fled to Lawrence County and later returned to the Rocky Plains. With the help of H. H. Bibb, she built another house about a mile from the original site. But too much blood had been spilled on the Plains and she was forced into exile. The Kaeiser Bottom then fell to ruin and nature started its long slow process of reclaiming the swamp that Kaeiser and his slaves had taken from her. The old wall at the original home site that the slaves built still stands and the Kaeiser spring still flows. The story lives on, for such things never die.

Historic references for this true story were provided by *Early Settlers of Alabama* by Col. James Edmonds Saunders; *Winston*, by Donald Dodd and Wynelle Dodd; and *The Free State of Winston* by Wesley Thompson; sites verification, B.J. Thomas.

Indians Hide in Sipsey

In the early part of the 1800s, white men learned of the Cherokee gold in north Georgia and Andrew Jackson was yearning to be president. This combination spelled doom for the Indians. They were destined to lose their land and one-fourth of them their lives. They could either sell their land to the government or be killed on it.

In that treaty with the United States Government, only some of those who were forced on the Trail of Tears were paid. The ones who remained behind hiding in the hills received nothing. A portion of the land in the Sipsey drainage of the present-day Bankhead National Forest was supposedly purchased from the Cherokees and Chickasaws; the North Alabama purchase in September 1816 had no western boundary properly described for the Cherokees and no eastern boundary for the Chickasaws. The lands taken were defined as having some five million acres. The same was not true for the Creeks; they were forced to give up their claims to the Sipsey by the Treaty of Fort Jackson in March 1814.

So who owns Bankhead National Forest? Does the government have title to it?

Many of the mixed-blood Cherokees refused to leave their ancestral home and fled to the hills. Everyone knows the story of the Cherokees in the Smokey Mountains, but few realize that many hid in Alabama. In the mountains of Jackson County, there is today a tribe of Cherokee Indians that have always been there. Last year, for the first time in 154 years, the government gave them their school money for that year, 932 of them. Also in Lawrence County, Alabama, mixed Scots Irish Cherokee students have had an Indian education program for some 30 years.

Other bands of Cherokees from the south side of the Tennessee River in the Decatur area fled into the Sipsey area of Lawrence, Winston, and Walker Counties. Where they went is not a mystery. The old family records show that many of the settlers in the forest were marrying Indians. Where were they coming from? They were supposed to be in Indian Territory of Oklahoma and other states west of the Mississippi River, but they had been hiding in the rugged isolated areas of the forest and Sipsey River drainage of the Black Warrior Mountains of North Alabama.

The Indian Removal Act was passed on May 28, 1830. From the year 1824 to 1850, Winston County was a part of Walker. So Indians fleeing moved into the mountainous areas of present-day Lawrence, Winston, and Walker Counties at the time of the removal come to what is now Winston County. They usually went to the least desirable and least inhabited part of the Sipsey area, for they were fugitives in hiding; many of the elders feared mentioning their Indian blood for fear of being force to unfamiliar lands west of the Mississippi River.

It would give a better insight into the plight of these people to understand they were under martial law of the War Department. The Indian people of Alabama, Mississippi, Tennessee, and Georgia could not openly reclaim their Indian ancestry until sections two through seven of the 1968 Civil Rights Act. Other Indian people across the United States were not even granted citizenship until 1924 and not allowed to vote until 1940. Some Native American children were beaten in school if heard speaking their native language, as directed by the United States Government which at the same time was trying to free the slaves.

If Kaeiser's slaves thought they were having it rough, they should have been born Red. They could have suffered right up until today the way Indians have been forced to. The Indians of North Alabama had every reason to hide because of the ethnic cleansing that was taking place under our United States laws and regulations of the time.

The Sipsey drainage was a rugged, isolated, and desolate place; much of the area was not settled until the 1850s, years after most of the surrounding area was settled. It was all that was left to the latecomers and they could buy it for 12 1/2 cents an acre.

In 1853, A.J. Thomas came to the Sipsey area of North Alabama from South Carolina. It has been told in the family that when he came to the area that there was an Indian village near where he settled. His great-grandson Charlie still lives on the old Thomas home site and remembers the story well and the general area of where that site was.

These Indians were living here in their village 27 years after they were marked for removal. The only way they could have survived that long without detection was by the white settlers protecting their secret hiding places. I had no reason to doubt the story and every reason to suspect it. If I could only get to the general area of the old village, the beech trees would tell me what I wanted to know.

All that stood in the way were the cotton mouth moccasins. They are big ones and the meanest snakes in the world. They are territorial and if you set foot in their place they will come after you. You never know where that place is until you are already in it. I have decided to go very carefully to the edge of the area anyway.

Had I any notion of what I was about to see I would have gone to it walking on cottonmouths stacked like cord wood. This tree alone is hard evidence that hanged the old story of A.J. Thomas from a legend to recorded history.

I have been in some deep woods and wild places, but as for a hiding place none will match the trackless swamps in the southern portion of the Sipsey area. The Indians must have always known it and found a few days of peace here before they became the Vanishing Americans.

There right where it should have been was a beech tree the size of a refrigerator. On two sides of that tree were Cherokee cryptic signs of the style you find at old village sites. On the other side of the tree was the carving of a white man. The carvings of the two are very near the same age and the white man dated the tree—1855.

Local Indian Families

This is a true story by researchers with the Eastern Band Cherokees supplemented with current knowledge. In many cases, it is your family history. The use of names is limited due to time and space but is sufficient to trace thousands of others if they desire to do so.

The story begins with the discovery of America. At first there were not too many of them. The Europeans came from across the ocean and settled along the coast. They were a pitiful lot. Alone in a new world, the Indians helped them survive.

Then more came and, with a foothold, increased in numbers and began to move deeper into the lands and forests. Some of the stronger moved deep into Indian country, taking Indian wives and living as Indians. One offspring of those mixed marriages was John Brown.

John Brown, while only a half-breed, was truly Indian. His white father made it possible for him, as an Indian, to see clearly both worlds that one day would come to conflict. He was literate and wise, a combination that elevated him to the rank of Chief of the Cherokees. His band of Cherokees lived on their ancestral lands in Marshall County, Alabama. The principal village was called Brown Village and its exact location is unknown.

Chief John Brown, as other Indians of stature, had three wives: Wati, Sara, and Selu (say-lou). He had many children and loved his people dearly. With the Revolutionary War, he was forced to make a decision that would be in the best interest of all his people. He had already seen his father's people infringing on his mother's land. The British promised him that if he would ally with them they would not allow the colonists to cross the mountains. He had no choice but to ally with England, for that was what was best for his people.

The British lost and Chief John Brown, as other chiefs in the nation, watched closely the formation of the new America. They greatly admired the Constitution created by the new nation and drafted one of their own patterned after it. Little did they realize how worthless the treaties with this new nation would be.

So the white man crossed the mountains. With this the Indians had to move farther from their ancestral grounds. It is not known how many children Chief John Brown had; it is known that the names of some of those children were Richard, David, Katherine, John, and William. These are the native sons and daughters of Alabama. The most historically recorded of these is Richard.

As the Cherokees began to spread out across Alabama, Richard had moved deep into the Creek Nation. Richard, like his father, had risen to the rank of chief and had founded a Cherokee village by the name of Turkey Town across the Coosa River from what is now Centre. Chief Richard Brown had received word that Creeks were going to attack his village. He requested help from Andrew Jackson who sent troops to Turkey Town. The Creeks did not show and while they were there Andrew Jackson enlisted Richard and his warriors into his army. It was from here that his next encounter with the Creeks would be—Horseshoe Bend.

After the Battle of Horseshoe Bend, Colonel Richard Brown moved his band deeper into the wilderness. Some of his people settled on Blackwater Creek near the present Town of Nauvoo. For some reason, the remaining Creeks sought refuge with Chief Richard Brown in north Walker and southern Winston Counties. History states that the Creeks numbered 200 and were led by Chief John Shannon. It was for these Indians that most of the creeks in the area were named, Browns Creek the most obvious.

It was in the 1820s that trouble was starting for the Cherokee. Gold was discovered by the whites in North Georgia. The Cherokee had known this for years but had not revealed it. The last name they had for gold translates *"yellow metal that makes white man crazy."* It was the gold, and Andrew Jackson's desire to be president, that made him turn against his friends, the Cherokees.

Occasionally such things arise from the past here in the Sipsey area of Alabama that astound even the Indians. Like a flint carved wooden medicine pipe elaborately decorated with stone hammered yellow metal; a metal that only made some white men crazy.

The Indians would have to leave. They were forced west on what was known as the Trail of Tears. One-fourth of them would die before they reached Oklahoma. Some could refuse to go and hid in the hills of North Alabama; they eventually assimilated into the general population, and are still here today. Those that did not seek the isolation of the hills and hollows of the Black Warrior Mountains would have to leave.

In the 1830s, the heartbreak of the removal would be too much to bear for another of Chief John Brown's sons. His name was also John, and he and his wife Hannah Brown would leave Morgan County and come to Winston County to be near his brother. The same was true for William. John and Hannah Brown settled near what is now Arley. It was there that they raised their family: Russell, Hugh, Elic, and Nancy. It was here that John would die and be buried in a hedge row.

John and Hannah would not be forgotten. They left several children that would stay and shape the new State of Alabama. Strangely enough it would be the daughter and not the sons that would be the best known in local history. Nancy Brown is mentioned throughout records in Walker County. Why would she be so widely known and not her brothers, Russell, Hugh, or Elic?

It is said in the family that one of the grandmothers was

Jefferson Thomas Sides
11/6/1864-9/16/1941

an herbal doctor that traveled around the area on horseback tending to the ailing. It could only have been Nancy. How else could a woman in those days become so widely known and respected to such an extreme that in some records they cannot remember the first name of the man she married, Elijah Sides. Nancy Brown died in 1886; she and Elijah Sides are buried in Old Zion Cemetery, on Alabama Highway 5, a few miles west of Jasper.

From this marriage came seven children, who remain for the most part in Walker County: Elizabeth Sides, who married R.J. Knight; David Sides, who married Elizabeth Harris; Buck Sides, who married Omia Bennett; Mary Sides, who married C.Y. Roberts; Jeff Sides, who married Sally Morgan; and Martha Sides, who married Abe Myers.

Nancy Sides' children have produced three generations of families in Walker County. There is now a seemingly endless list of names like Myers, Sides, Knight, Tidwell, Boshell, Cagle, King, Richardson, Garrison, Clay, Ferguson, Hodges, Roberts, Calloway, Cook, Davis, Leonard, Dill, Castleberry, Norris, Cooper, Manasco, Blanton, Odom, and Nichols. This is from the first descendants of Nancy alone and we have not even mentioned the Browns. Even with the Browns included, the list would only be the tip of the iceberg.

Another piece of history came to light: the instruction sheet to a form that Jeff Sides filed for government money. I find it sad and irritating. The story behind this seemingly worthless piece of paper: When Jeff's ancestors' were moved west, the government paid only a few pennies per acre for the land they took from the Cherokee.

The Cherokees who refused to leave or didn't were forced to leave receiving nothing. It was 70 years later that the courts ordered the government to pay the Eastern Cherokees for their land. Jeff or none of his relatives, Cherokees in Walker or Winston Counties, ever received it.

What of all those descendants of the other Cherokees that were with them? What of the 200 Creeks? It may never be known now. Yet almost every day things come out into the open that reveal beyond words the Indian heritage of the people of Walker, Winston, and Lawrence Counties.

211

Back Row L-R: *Millard, William Amos, Sary, Delie and Willie.* Front Row L-R: *Ruby, Mattie, Mary Tennessee Garrison Spillers (3/4 Cherokee) and Will Spillers. All of Will and Mary's children are 3/8 Cherokee.*

The old trunks and boxes in attics in the area contain a wealth of information that should be in the county library. Never destroy those old photographs, letters, or handwritten books. If you don't want to take them to the library, let someone else evaluate them.

We may never know much of the past history of Mary Tennessee Garrison Spillers. Her son, Amos Spillers, second from the left, was the first conservation officer in the Bankhead National Forest.

Now throughout Lawrence, Walker, and Winston Counties, hundreds, possibly thousands of Americans sit down to the traditional turkey dinner on Thanksgiving Day and never suspect that they are a part of both pilgrims and the history they are honoring; these are the Celtic Indian people of the Sipsey drainage of the Black Warrior Mountains of North Alabama.

CONCLUSION

Most people have no idea how severe the fight was to save the Sipsey Wilderness Area; the battle for the original Sipsey lasted some 15 years. Finally, the United States Congress passed the Eastern Wilderness Areas Act of 1974 which contained 12,726 acres in the Sipsey Wilderness Area; United States President Gerald Ford signed the Eastern Wilderness legislation on January 3, 1975, and the official dedication was on May 17, 1975. At last, we in North Alabama had our own little wilderness area, but it was not without many struggles in our national congress, in the regional agencies of the forest service, at the state level, and down to local grassroots campaigns.

With one battle won in the Sipsey Wilderness Area, another struggle to save additional areas in Bankhead Forest lasted another 14 years. Clear cutting old growth hardwoods and replacing them with fast growing commercial pines was at the heart of the fight; it appeared the only way to stop clear cutting was in the form of additional wilderness in Bankhead.

The forest service was accelerating clear cutting in order to eliminate other areas for wilderness; it appeared the only way to stop the destruction of Bankhead's old growth hardwoods by the United States Forest Service was to create more wilderness areas in the forest. United States Congressman Ronnie G. Flippo of Florence became the point man in the Sipsey Wilderness Addition, but the fight on a local level became much more intense with even death threats.

On April 1, 1982, Ronnie Flippo introduced legislation into the United States House of Representatives to enlarge the Sipsey Wilderness Area by some 30,000 acres; Flippo's bill failed to get the senatorial support from Howell Heflin and died. In spite of staunch opposition of the timber barons and forest service, United States Congressman Ronnie G. Flippo had received 95% of the Lawrence County vote for his seat in congress; Flippo and Heflin finally reached a compromise with 13,260 of wilderness addition and another 5,000 acres included in the National Wild and Scenic Rivers System which included the upper drainage of the Sipsey Wilderness Area.

According to John Randolph's book *The Battle for Alabama's Wilderness*, page 185, "*And though it seemed hard to believe, indeed it was. On October 28, 1988, President Ronald Reagan signed into law P.L. 100-547, the Sipsey Wild and Scenic River and Alabama Additions Act of 1988, and a Sipsey Wilderness expansion of 13,260 acres became reality.*" Ronnie Flippo attended the Sipsey Wilderness expansion ceremony on April 14, 1989. Finally, another long fight was over and North Alabama was to be a premier wilderness site in the eastern United States, but the clear cutting of our native old growth hardwoods and the conversion to commercial pine thickets did not stop.

The United States Forest Service was one of the strongest advocates against creating the wilderness in Bankhead Forest; they did everything in their power to prevent the area from being designated wilderness and tried to discourage everyone from even trying to get the area set aside. The forest service wanted to be able to clear cut every acre of the forest for timber production and pine stand conversion; corporate timber interests had the forest service in their back pocket and their fight was all about padding the pockets of the timber barons—MONEY.

The efforts of people like Jim and Ruth Manasco in the first wilderness and Charles Borden in the Sipsey Wilderness addition were instrumental in the preservation of our Bankhead

Forest areas to be protected for our future generations to enjoy. In addition, many other people contributed their time and energy to save Bankhead Forest from destruction by clear cutting and at the same time preserve wilderness, but one individual stands out in the slowing and near stoppage of clear cutting of our forest, and that person is Lamar Marshall.

Lamar Marshall faced death threats, but stood with a backbone of steel against the United States Forest Service and the corporate timber industry. Through Lamar's efforts, places like Indian Tomb Hollow, High Town Path, and Kinlock cultural area received some protection from degradation by forest service activities. However, for these Indian heritage and cultural sites, I strongly encourage our younger generations to stay vigilant; do not allow the United States Forest Service to destroy our aboriginal heritage sites in William B. Bankhead National Forest.

For the young folks that were not involved in the fight for the Sipsey Wilderness Area and Native sites which are considered Traditional Cultural Properties, it is hard to explain how the government bureaucracy of the forest service could be so distrustful and deceptive. For those who trust the forest service today, just remember all the treaties with American Indian people that were broken by the United States Government; nothing has changed. We must remain diligent and aware of the previous actions of the United States Forest Service because of the minerals that lay under our public lands of Bankhead Forest; there are trillions of dollars of tar sands that cover a large area of North Alabama and lay under the Sipsey drainage area.

Beware of governmental agencies like the forest service and industrial power brokers that wear you down and find the right time to attack; their motives appear to be about control and money. Our future fellow Americans are our children, grandchildren, and great-grandchildren; they deserve the best legacy that we can leave them. It is not in concrete and steel, but the wild places in our ancestral landscape where peace and tranquility abound.

INDEX

A

aboriginal 1, 6, 39, 72, 81, 116, 138, 215
Addison 33
Alabama Chinquapin 186
Alabama Conservancy 35, 37, 40, 42, 50
Alabama Croton 167, 168
Alabama Ecological Society 50
Alexander, Fran 39, 40
Alexander Motorway 116
Allen, Jim 44
Allen, Ralph 39, 40
Appalachian Mountains 5
Apuleii Platonici 165
Arizona 32
Ashbank 12
Ashcraft, Sarah Susanna 22
Asherbranner Cemetery 143
Auburn University 27, 50, 57
Audubon Society 40, 41, 50
Aunt Jenny 127, 128, 199

B

Bachman's warbler 112
Bankhead Amateur Radio Club 88
Bankhead Forest 5, 7, 8, 10, 25, 30, 32, 33, 34, 50, 60, 61, 64, 69, 72,
    110, 118, 122, 124, 125, 126, 128, 141, 189, 200, 213, 214, 215
Bankhead Monitor 38
Bankhead National Forest 1, 5, 14, 16, 26, 30, 32, 38, 40, 41, 50, 55, 60,
    64, 65, 67, 70, 80, 81, 92, 108, 115, 129, 130, 142, 146, 191, 199,
    204, 212, 215
barred owl 183, 184
Basham Shelter 142
Battle of Horseshoe Bend 209
Bear Bottoms 118
Bearce, Denny N. 50
Beaver Creek Wilderness Area 70
Beavers Sawmill 145

218

C

Q

R

228

T

Y

Bluewater Publications is a multi-faceted publishing company capable of meeting all of your reading and publishing needs. Our two-fold aim is to:

1) Provide the market with educationally enlightening and inspiring research and reading materials.

2) Make the opportunity of being published available to any author and or researcher who desires to be published.

We are passionate about preserving history, whether through the re-publishing of an out-of-print classic or by publishing the research of historians and genealogists. Bluewater Publications is the *Peoples' Choice Publisher*.

To learn more about Rickey Butch Walker or for information about how you can be published through Bluewater Publications, please visit:

www.BWPublications.com

Also check Amazon.com to purchase any of the books that we publish.

Confidently Preserving Our Past,
Bluewater Publications

www.ingramcontent.com/pod-product-compliance
Lightning Source LLC
Chambersburg PA
CBHW020530270326
41927CB00006B/514